How to Ace the National Geographic Bee

Official Study Guide

Fourth Edition

by

Stephen F. Cunha

NATIONAL GEOGRAPHIC

Washington, D.C.

For information about special discounts for bulk purchases, please contact National Geographic Books Special Sales: ngspecsales@ngs.org

For rights or permissions inquiries, please contact National Geographic Books Subsidiary Rights: ngbookrights@ngs.org

Cover design by David M. Seager

The text type is set in New Caledonia; headlines are set in Clarendon.

All questions and place-names were accurate and current at the date of their actual use in the National Geographic Bee.

Trade paperback ISBN 978-1-4263-0986-1
Library ISBN 978-1-4263-0985-4

Printed in the United States of America

15/WOR/3

Contents

Foreword

In fourth grade, I participated in my first geography bee. I placed second and was disappointed, but I didn't give up. I continued to study in preparation for the following year's competition. I won the school competition the second time around and qualified for the state bee. A second-place finish and two state bee titles later, I found myself in the headquarters of the National Geographic Society, along with nine other students from across the United States. We stepped onto the stage of the Grosvenor Auditorium to thunderous applause. During the competition, we answered questions about topics ranging from culture to current events to landforms. When the dust finally settled, I was crowned the 23rd National Geographic Bee champion.

When you first heard about the National Geographic Bee, you probably thought that it was the exclusive domain of nerds with thick glasses and pocket protectors who knew the capitals of a few countries. Well, think again. Geography bees can be very exciting! You may be surprised at how diverse the participants are and how interesting the questions can be. It's not just about naming countries and capital cities—contestants answer questions about almost anything that can be found on Earth. Some of the more obscure questions I have heard during my time as a contestant have related to elephant-dancing festivals, pingos, and relations between Iran and Turkmenistan.

These competitions require you to think globally to answer a question. A good example is the fourth question of the 2011 National Geographic Bee championship round: "Tungurahua, which means 'throat of fire' in Quechua, is one of the most active volcanoes in what South American country?" I knew from my study of linguistics that Quechua was the language of the Inca. Drawing on this, and also knowing that a string of volcanoes in central and southern Ecuador is known as the Avenue of the Volcanoes, my answer was Ecuador. The fact that my opponent missed this question gave me a 4-3 lead in the championship round. I then held on to win the competition. Many other such questions require you to draw on information from many different fields of study. It also takes a long time to accumulate the knowledge necessary to place high at the state bee and make it to the national competition. I have participated in four school bees, three state bees, two national bees, and one national final round. I won the National Geographic Bee in my fourth year of competition.

If you are interested in the world around you and want to learn more, I encourage you to test your geographic knowledge in a geography bee. Be prepared to work hard for several years in order to reach the highest level of the competition, and don't give up. Whether you make it to the national finals or not, you will walk away from the competition with the satisfaction that you have vastly improved your understanding of geography. With this knowledge, you will be better equipped to understand the events around the world that shape your future. The fact that you are reading this book is a good first step. I hope you have many more enjoyable moments as you dive into the vast body of knowledge that is geography.

Tine Valencic
Champion
2011 National Geographic Bee

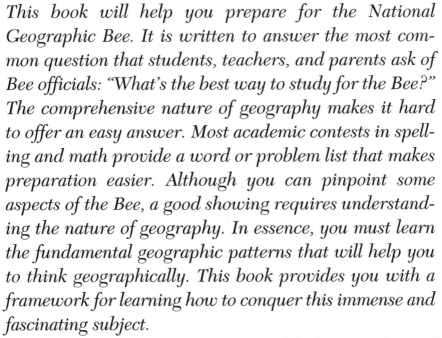

I like Geography best, he said, because your mountains and rivers know the secret. Pay no attention to boundaries.
—BRIAN ANDREAS,
AMERICAN POET

Introduction

This book will help you prepare for the National Geographic Bee. It is written to answer the most common question that students, teachers, and parents ask of Bee officials: "What's the best way to study for the Bee?" The comprehensive nature of geography makes it hard to offer an easy answer. Most academic contests in spelling and math provide a word or problem list that makes preparation easier. Although you can pinpoint some aspects of the Bee, a good showing requires understanding the nature of geography. In essence, you must learn the fundamental geographic patterns that will help you to think geographically. This book provides you with a framework for learning how to conquer this immense and fascinating subject.

The first chapter explores the world of geography and explains why it is so important to study the subject. Then the origin and purpose of the Bee as well as the structure and format of the contest are discussed. Chapter 3 provides tips on how and what to study for the Bee. Chapter 4 tells you how to look for clues in the questions and use the study tips to come up with the correct answers, then provides lots of real Bee questions so you can test yourself. Bee winners offer advice and inspiration in Chapter 5, and resources that will help you study are evaluated in Chapter 6. The Note to Teachers discusses various initiatives and support groups available for teaching geography more effectively and helping students prepare for the Bee.

Although we live at the dawn of the digital age, Thomas Jefferson's ideal regarding the truly educated person still stands:

> In the elementary schools will be taught reading, writing, common arithmetic, and general notions of geography. In the district colleges, ancient and modern languages, geography fully, a higher degree of numerical arithmetic…and the elementary principles of navigation.
>
> —Thomas Jefferson to M. Correa da Serra (1817)

Jefferson believed that a balanced curriculum produced more capable and enlightened citizens than one that focused on just one or two subjects. Although Jefferson never booted up a computer to surf the Web or e-mail his friends, he correctly forecast the value of exercising all parts of the human brain. Were he alive today, he would be pleased by your interest in geography and in the world around you.

What kind of young people enter the Bee? The Society's staff and those of us who work with them have about 20 years of data on this very subject. We find that Bee kids play instruments and compete in sports. Many run for student government and join school clubs. Some tour the globe with their parents; others journey mostly in their imaginations. Some kids say their favorite subject is math; others say literature, physical education, or even—gasp—geography. There are tall and short kids, big and small kids, funny kids, and very, very serious kids. Bee kids hail from our largest cities and smallest towns (the first national champion attended a one-room schoolhouse in rural Kansas). Some attend public or private schools; others are homeschooled. What unites them is a natural curiosity about our world.

This book can help you be more competitive at every level of the contest. But advancing through the rounds should not be the only reason to enter the Bee or to study these chapters. The real benefit comes from learning what geography is all about, and that alone will enrich your life forever. You'll be amazed how geography makes you a better reader, a more knowledgeable historian, a better mathematician, and a more versatile scientist. Geography links other subjects into a seamless whole whose sum greatly exceeds its parts. Most important, studying geography will help you become a more sensitive and aware citizen of our global community.

Let the adventure begin!

CHAPTER 1

The Why of Where: Defining Geography

From space I saw Earth—indescribably beautiful with the scars of national boundaries gone.
—ASTRONAUT MUHAMMAD AHMAD FARIS, SYRIA (1988)

Imagine captaining a 17th-century merchant ship with a crew of 200 and a cargo hold stuffed with exotic goods from the Far East. You are London-bound to exchange your booty for gold coins and more shipping contracts from anxious merchants. Gazing across the Indian Ocean at sunrise, you take stock of the possible hazards that threaten success: pirates, sudden storms, rocky coastlines, and even mutiny. But the biggest danger of all is veering off course into an endless sea because you cannot plot your location accurately on the map.

Before John Harrison developed a special clock called the marine chronometer in the mid-1700s, sailors could not pinpoint their longitude—their location east or west of the prime meridian. Captains routinely lost hundreds of men and tons of cargo to starvation and storms while searching for a place to land. In Dava Sobel's wonderful book Longitude, *the author describes a dozen disasters,* including that of Admiral Sir Clowdisley Shovell. The admiral lost four of his five warships and 2,000 troops in 1707 after misjudging his longitude in the Scilly Isles, off the southwestern tip of England. Adrift in dense fog, the ships "pricked themselves on rocks and went down like stones." Yikes!

Fortunately, Harrison's ingenious clock enabled navigators to determine longitude by comparing the time of day on board ship with noon in Greenwich, England, which was (and still is) located on the prime meridian (0° longitude). Because latitude—the distance north or south of the Equator—was easy to calculate by observing the stars, sailors could now see where their latitude and longitude intersected on the map and determine their exact geographic location in an open ocean where there are no landmarks. (You'll learn more about latitude and longitude in Chapter 3.)

Early continental explorers also suffered when they lacked geographical information. Poor Hannibal crossed the Alps in the wrong time of year and nearly froze to death. Lewis and Clark almost perished in the mountains of Idaho and Montana because they didn't know how vast the Rocky Mountains were. And what were those Vikings thinking when they attempted to grow barley in Iceland a thousand years ago?

Knowing where places are located is an important first step to learning geography and enjoying the Bee. Fortunately for us, using maps and finding latitude and longitude are much easier today than during poor Sir Clowdisley Shovell's lifetime.

However, geography is much more than places on a map. In the words of Alexander Graham Bell, one of the founders of the

National Geographic Society, geography is "the world and all that is in it." Place-names such as Brazil, Stockholm, Mount Everest, and Yangtze River are to geography what the alphabet is to reading. They open the gate for boundless and lifelong learning. Knowing where places are on a map is important, but the real heart of geography is understanding why people settle in a particular place, who their neighbors are, how they make a living, why they dress and speak the way they do, and what they do for fun. Developing this sense of place will raise a flat map to life.

Geographers investigate our global climate, landforms, economies, political systems, human cultures, and migration patterns. They are concerned not just with where something is located, but also with why it is there and how it relates to other things. A good geographer knows how to combine this information from many different sources and how to identify patterns that can help us understand our complex world. Geography explains why your grandmother moved to Tucson (warm and dry climate), how oil from Kuwait reaches Italy (by way of the Suez Canal), where tropical rain forests grow (near the Equator), who faces toward Mecca as they pray (Muslims), and which continent is the most populated (Asia). In a nutshell, geography is the "Why of Where" science that blends and enriches history, literature, mathematics, and science.

Although place-names of the world are now thoroughly mapped and available in atlases, maps, books, and even online, knowing where you are and the geographic characteristics of that place are just as important today as in earlier times.

Understanding people and environments influences the location of everything from Walmarts to hospitals to software manufacturing plants. City planners need population projections and environmental data before they can approve plans to build housing developments, office buildings, and shopping centers. Engineers must study water resources and the lay of the land before starting any project (even a small hill or creek can greatly increase construction costs). Imagine trying to advertise a new product without knowing the composition (Hispanic, African American, Asian, European), age structure (teenagers or grandparents), and economic characteristics (farmers, factory workers, or professionals) of the people you want to buy it. Highway construction cannot proceed until facts about climate, soil, vegetation, and the number of people who will drive the proposed route are considered. Each day, kids everywhere awake in sheets of woven Egyptian cotton, pull on clothes stitched in Bangladesh, wolf down bananas grown in Central America, and grab schoolbooks printed in Singapore to board buses assembled in Michigan from parts made in Japan and Germany.

For more than a decade, the growth of our global society—the rising dependence of nations upon each other for trade and security—has made geographical studies more important than ever. Acronyms and abbreviations, such as NAFTA, GATT, EU, and WTO, are heard on the evening news. Schools from Alaska to Zambia stress second-language and culture studies to better prepare their students not just for a global economy but also for a more crowded planet where migration, tourism, and the

Internet connect our global family more each day. The global war on terrorism further underscores the great importance of more fully understanding the people of the world, how they live, what they believe, and the environment and resources we share.

Whether you are the secretary of state for the United States or the secretary of your class, knowing geography will help you understand the world.

To Bee or not to Bee,
that is the question.
—SHAKESPEARE (SORT OF)

CHAPTER **2**

Bee Basics: Understanding the Contest

This chapter marches through the annual Bee calendar from registration to the national finals. It explains who is eligible to participate and the format at the school, state, and national levels. (It is important to note that although the Bee provides an instruction booklet to each registered school, the booklet contains recommended procedures only. Schools sometimes have to make adjustments to fit their needs.) Understanding how the Bee works and following the advice at the end of the chapter will help you relax, have fun, and perform better.

REGISTRATION

Registering is easy. Although only principals may register their schools, students (or their parents) can often stir teachers and principals into action. Check with school officials to see if your school is entered for the upcoming Bee or look for your school on our Web site under the registration link. If you are a middle school student who rotates among classes, the social studies teacher is your best bet, followed by the principal. Schools must register *each* year by the deadline (usually October 15). More information on Bee registration appears on page 121 and on our Web site: www.nationalgeographic.com/geobee.

ELIGIBILITY

All U.S. schools with any of the grades four through eight may register for the Bee. Students enrolled in a conventional public or private school may not compete as part of a homeschool Bee. Homeschooling associations may register to have a county or areawide Bee for homeschoolers in their area. A student may compete in a magnet school Bee only if enrolled full-time at the magnet school. Parents and teachers must pay close attention to these details to prevent a disqualification.

Students who are not over the age of 15 by September 1 of that school year may participate. The Bee is an open contest that does not separate students into age or grade-level categories. There must be a minimum of six student participants in a school to hold a school-level competition. Students may participate in no more than five years of the Bee.

SCHOOL-LEVEL BEES

In mid November, the Society mails Bee packets to each registered school. The packet contains the suggested procedures, the question booklet, a medal for the winner, and a Certificate of Participation for each student who takes part. School officials then select the days for their Bee, so long as the competition falls within the dates established by the Society—normally anytime between mid-November and mid-January.

School Bees are the responsibility of the schools. Their decisions are final. These Bees are usually broken into a Preliminary Competition, which normally takes place in individual classrooms, and the Final Competition, which is often held in the school assembly room (cafeteria, auditorium, gym, etc.).

Preliminary Competition

These rounds usually require an oral response. A teacher or other moderator reads the questions aloud. You will be asked one question per round and will have 15 seconds to answer each question. To keep the contest moving, you are allowed to ask to have a question repeated or a word spelled only two times during the Preliminary Competition. Such a request to the moderator must be made immediately.

Once the question has been repeated or the word spelled, you will have the remainder of your 15 seconds to answer the question. You must start to give your answer before the 15-second time limit is up. If you do not answer within the allotted time, the moderator will say, "Time," give the correct answer, and move on to the next student. One point is awarded for each correct response; a pass is counted as an incorrect response. There is no penalty for mispronunciations (or misspellings, in the event of a written response) so long as the moderator can determine you know the correct answer. The student with the most correct answers wins the chance to advance to the Final Round.

Tiebreakers

If there are ties in determining the finalists, officials will use a series of Preliminary Competition Tiebreaker Questions. Everyone involved begins with a clean slate—no hits and no misses. Students get the same question and write their answers on the paper provided. Again, there is no penalty for misspellings so long as the moderator can determine that the correct answer has been given. Questioning continues until the tie or ties have been broken.

Final Competition

The Final Competition consists of a Final Round and a Championship Round. If you are lucky enough to advance to this level, you may find yourself on a stage in the school auditorium. As with any contest or game, the pressure builds as you progress up the ladder. Expect some bright lights and audience noise, ranging from restrained gasps to thunderous applause.

In addition to the round-robin oral questions in the Preliminary Competition, the Final Round includes questions that require written responses (students are simultaneously asked the same question and respond by writing their answers on the paper provided). Other questions may involve graphs, maps, or photographs. If so, you will be given a copy of the visual to study up close before answering the question. But the biggest difference between the Preliminary Competition and the Final Round is that students are eliminated after giving their second incorrect answer. Once the third-place winner has been determined, the remaining two students advance to the Championship Round.

Championship Round

In the Championship Round the two contestants start with a clean slate. Both are asked the same questions simultaneously and given 15 seconds to write their answers. The moderator then asks the students for their answers. The student with the most correct answers wins the school Bee. Tiebreaker questions may be necessary to determine the winner. The champion receives a prize and certificate from the National Geographic Society, and every student who entered the school Bee receives a Certificate of Participation.

QUALIFYING TEST

To advance to the state Bee as a representative of his or her school, the school winner must take the written Qualifying Test. This test should be given in a quiet location in the school building. It must be monitored by a teacher who is not a parent or guardian of the school Bee winner. There are about 70 multiple-choice questions, covering the entire range of geographic inquiry, including a set that pertains to a map, table, or graph. There is a time limit of one hour. When time is up, the teacher administering the test must sign the certification statement on the answer sheet and mail it to the National Geographic Society. The test must be received by the Society no later than January 31 of the year of the test. Tests received after that date will not be graded. Faxes are not accepted.

The National Geographic Society scores one Qualifying Test from each participating school. The top 100 students (more if there are ties) from each of the 50 states, the District of Columbia, the Department of Defense Dependents Schools, and the Atlantic and Pacific territories compete in the State Bees. The National Geographic Society appoints state Bee coordinators to coordinate this portion of the contest. In early March, Society officials notify the teachers of the students who qualify for the state competition.

STATE-LEVEL BEES

The state Bees are usually held in early April. An adult must accompany each student to the State Bee. In most cases this is a teacher, parent, or legal guardian. Other adults may substitute with school approval. Expect the Bee to begin with an opening assembly jam-packed with all 100 state finalists, officials, teachers, and a zillion family members. The room is abuzz with excitement and nervous anticipation.

The contestants break into five groups of 20 students. The seating and room assignments are determined by random drawing before the Bee. Just as in the school-level competition, there are preliminary, final, and championship rounds (and tiebreakers if necessary). The Final and Championship Rounds are held in front of a large audience and are very exciting. Some rounds will include questions that require written responses on a sheet of paper. You should also expect questions that require interpreting information from a visual. This may be a photograph, illustration, map, satellite photo (from Google Earth), data table, or graph that is displayed on a large screen. You will be given a copy of the visual to study up close before answering the question. Once the Bee is under way, you will impress yourself with how many questions you can answer correctly! The same procedure that is recommended to schools for determining the school-level winners is used to determine the state champions. The winner of each state Bee wins a trip to Washington, D.C., to compete in the national-level Bee.

THE NATIONAL-LEVEL BEE

State Bee winners meet at the headquarters of the National Geographic Society, in Washington, D.C., in late May to compete for the title of national champion. The format for the national-level preliminary competition is similar to that of the previous levels of the Bee except that the questions are harder and there are more rounds involving visuals, such as photographs, maps, and graphs. The top ten winners of the Preliminary Competition compete in the Final Round. Starting in 2012, the format of the Final Round will be different from the earlier levels of the Bee. More information will be made available to State Bee winners. Alex Trebek, host of TV's *JEOPARDY!*, has moderated the Final and Championship Rounds since 1989. It's always fun to follow along and see how many questions you can answer; check the Bee Web site for local broadcast information. The top three finishers take home college scholarships. The total prize and scholarship monies awarded at the school, state, and national levels make the Bee one of the richest academic competitions for schoolkids on Earth.

THE CANADIAN GEOGRAPHY CHALLENGE

The Canadian equivalent of the National Geographic Bee also features a series of competitions at the school, provincial or territorial, and national levels that are designed to test students' knowledge and skills in geography.

Currently there are two grade levels to the Challenge: Level 1 for grades four to six and Level 2 for grades seven and above. Level 2 competitors must be under the age of 16 as of June 30 (the end of the school year in which the Challenge takes place). Teachers register online for the Challenge; any number of students or classes within a school may compete. All registered schools receive an online instruction booklet, question and answer booklet, and prizes. The information is available in English and French.

The competition for Level 1 students ends at the school level. When the top student has been determined at the school level in Level 2 (this must be determined by the end of February), he or she will write the provincial/territorial online test to see if they will be invited to the national final. The top student in each province and territory will be recognized with a prize. The highest scoring students from this competition compete in the National Final in April. The top three scorers are declared the Canadian National Champions and receive scholarships.

BEE GREAT: ADVICE TO CONTESTANTS

The following list is the result of more than a decade of "Bee-ing" with students, teachers, and parents. Although my experience has been mostly at the state level, these tips will help at any level in almost any type of competition. They are included here to help make the Bee a truly memorable and fun event.

Relax! Cramming hurts your brain

The evening before and the morning of the Bee are prime times to relax, play with your dog, and bike ride with a sibling or friend. Don't stay up the night before conversing with owls while attempting to cram in a few last-minute facts. This contest is fun, so rest up and dream of faraway lands.

Set aside part of each day to prepare for the Bee. Remember that geography is an integrative subject that takes time to learn and appreciate. Avoid flipping flash cards on the way to the Bee. (Several times I have seen parents quizzing students just moments before the Bee!) This adds tension that can detract from the quality of your performance and your enjoyment of the competition.

Healthy body, healthy mind

Whether you live in Paris, Pyongyang, or Philadelphia, the best advice is to stay fit, eat a balanced diet, and avoid spending so much time hunting for facts online or looking things up in books that your physical fitness declines. A healthy body houses a sharper and more capable mind.

Many students at every level of the Bee find that eating before the contest is a difficult idea to stomach. Yet your brain is a big muscle, and to keep it working at full throttle requires high-octane fuel. That is to say, CHOW DOWN BEFORE THE BEE! Don't arrive hungry. An empty stomach will make any jitters you have feel much worse. This problem does not affect every student, but if you know that big events—even the fun ones—make it difficult to eat, then here is some food for thought.

First, eat a well-balanced dinner the night before the Bee. This way, unless your stomach is the size of a thimble, you'll have calories in your tank at least through noon the following day. Second, eat at least a small breakfast that includes some juice and something solid, such as fruit, carbohydrates (toast, muffins, cereal), or eggs. Try to avoid greasy and high-fat foods, as they are harder to digest and can make your tummy do backflips.

Dress for success

Although this is a special event, you don't need to rent a tux or a frilly evening gown. Even ties and dresses are rare. Most kids pull on something comfortable. Pants or a skirt with a clean shirt or blouse are a good choice. Of course, you'll want to look neat—advancing to the finals at any level could land you onstage.

Take a deep breath

It's easy to panic when you hear a question that freaks you out! "Oh no, I can't remember the largest city on Mars!" Forgetting to breathe or taking several gasps is a natural reaction. If this occurs, relax, take a deep breath, collect your thoughts, and then look for clues in the question that will help you figure out the correct answer. Remember, you have 15 seconds (except in the national finals) to answer. Believe it or not, that's a long time! Failing to take in oxygen will make it more difficult to think and will increase that feeling of alarm!

Listen to every question in each round

When competing in the oral rounds, listen to every question and every answer. You may pick up clues that will help you come up with the right answer when it's your turn.

Stand by your first answer

Unless you are certain of an error, stick with the first answer that comes to mind. Believe it or not, studies show that students who change their answers or get stuck trying to choose between two answers usually select a less accurate choice the second time.

Ignore your friends

While you're competing, don't look at people you know, especially just before and during your turn. Ask your friends, teacher, parents, and other family members to make themselves invisible by sitting as far away as possible. Also, tell them to photograph you *after* the Bee, not while you are trying to remember which country borders Zimbabwe on the east. (Mozambique, of course!)

Speak loudly and write with a big stick

Make your answers known in very decisive ways. Speak in a loud, clear voice. When a written answer is required, write clearly in LARGE, BOLD LETTERS. The teacher/moderator must be able to understand your answer and read your handwriting.

Remember: It is impossible to fail in the Bee. Just by taking part you are already a success!

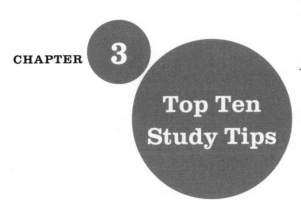

CHAPTER 3

Top Ten Study Tips

*All the rivers
run into the sea;
yet the sea is not full;
Unto the place
from whence
the rivers come,
thither they return
again.*
—ECCLESIASTES

*The ten trusty tips outlined in this chapter will help you
"Bee" ready. This powerful advice has been assembled
over many years from students just like you. A small
army of teachers added their two cents' worth, too.*

*Don't expect to learn everything about geography in
just one school year. Remember that you are eligible to
enter the Bee from the fourth through the eighth grade.
No one expects a fourth grader to know as much as an
eighth grader, but it's not impossible. Susannah Batko-
Yovino was only a sixth grader when she became the
national champion in 1990! By participating each year,
you will increase your knowledge of geography and self-
confidence. These ten study tips will teach you the basics
and how to build on them to recognize geographic
patterns. You'll be thinking like a geographer in no time!*

TIP #1   Choose Your Tools

Getting started in geography is easy if you have the right tools. Spending a part of each day with these tools will expand your world in a hurry. A few pointers on using these are presented here. Advice about specific products and where to find them appears in Chapter 6.

A large **WORLD MAP** should be in every home. Concentrate first on learning the continents, oceans, and largest islands. Then focus on countries, capital cities, and major physical features (such as mountain ranges, lakes, and rivers), gradually adding other places and features to your vocabulary. Hang your world map next to your bed or on the closet door. Put smaller maps of each continent around your house. Position one in the bathroom so you can learn the countries of Africa while brushing your teeth. Laminated map place mats let you explore Italy while slurping spaghetti. You can also tape maps behind the front seat of your family car and visit South America on the way to school.

A good **ATLAS** is the next essential tool. These come in all sizes, with many excellent and reasonably priced volumes to match your skill level. Be sure to use one that is less than five years old so that it includes important name updates.

Look for three other features when choosing an atlas. First, it should have both physical maps (emphasizing natural features) and political maps (emphasizing country boundaries and cities). Second, make sure it includes an index (or gazetteer) that alphabetically lists place-names that appear on the maps. This will help you find unfamiliar locations. Finally, look for text that includes information about each continent, country, and world region (such as Southeast Asia or Middle America), plus a section on geographic comparisons (longest rivers, largest cities, etc.).

BLANK OUTLINE MAPS are the third tool. These black-and-white line maps outline the continents and countries. Important physical features such as major rivers and mountain ranges may also appear. See Chapter 6 for tips on finding the maps online. Practice labeling countries, cities, rivers, mountains, and other geographic information as you learn it. Always start with the most obvious features, then add more detailed information as you progress. Blank maps are a great way to quiz yourself.

A **GEOGRAPHY REFERENCE BOOK** is another important tool. Although maps and atlases help you learn where Mongolia, Mauna Loa, and other places are located, a good geography reference book explains *why* they are located there, *who* lives there, *what* they do, and *how* the landscape came to be. These books usually arrange information in alphabetical order either by single topic (Agriculture, Alluvial Fan, Avalanche), or by category (Earth Science, Population, Wildlife). The most helpful ones enrich the text with numerous maps, photographs, charts and graphs, and a glossary of terms. A good reference book takes you to the next level of geographic learning by bringing maps to life. This marks the point where memorization evolves into real geographic exploration and discovery!

GOOGLE EARTH rounds out your tool kit. Learning to maneuver about and interpret Google satellite images will help you to visualize and build the mental maps described in Tip #4.

Learn the Language of Maps

A good map is worth a thousand pictures. Expert map readers can absorb oceans of geographic information in a short time. But to understand all that a map can tell you, you must first learn the language of maps.

LATITUDE and **LONGITUDE** are the imaginary lines that divide Earth's surface into a grid. Under this system, both latitude and longitude are measured in terms of the 360 degrees of a circle. The latitude and longitude of a place are its **COORDINATES**. Coordinates mark the **ABSOLUTE LOCATION** of a place. Understanding coordinates, you can use a map to locate any point on Earth.

Latitude is the distance north or south of the **EQUATOR**, the line of 0° latitude that divides the Earth into two equal halves called hemispheres. The top half is the **NORTHERN HEMISPHERE**, and the bottom half is the **SOUTHERN HEMISPHERE**. Lines of latitude are also called **PARALLELS** because they circle the Earth without ever touching each other. From the Equator we measure latitude north and south to the Poles. The **NORTH POLE** is located at 90°N latitude, and the **SOUTH POLE** is located at 90°S latitude.

There are other important parallels that you should learn. The parallel of latitude 23½° north of the Equator is called the **TROPIC OF CANCER**, and the parallel 23½° south of the Equator is the **TROPIC OF CAPRICORN**. The region between these two parallels is called the **TROPICS**. The **SUBTROPICS** are the zones located between $23^{1/2}°$ and about 40° north and south of the Equator.

The parallel of latitude $66^{1/2}°$ north of the Equator is called the **ARCTIC CIRCLE**, and the parallel $66^{1/2}°$ south of the Equator is the **ANTARCTIC CIRCLE**. The region between $66^{1/2}°$N and 90°N is called the Arctic; the region between $66^{1/2}°$S and 90°S is called the Antarctic. Both regions can simply be called polar.

Longitude is the distance east or west of the **PRIME MERIDIAN**, the point of 0° longitude. This is also the starting place for measuring distance both east and west around the globe. Lines of longitude are called **MERIDIANS**. They also circle Earth, but connect with each other at the Poles.

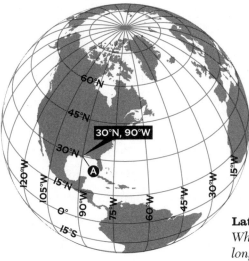

Latitude and Longitude
When used together, latitude and longitude form a grid that provides a system for determining the exact, or absolute, location of every place on Earth. For example, the absolute location of point A is 30°N, 90°W.

We also use the coordinate system to determine direction. When you face the North Pole (90°N), the sun rises to your right (east) and sets to your left (west). The south is behind you. These four points—north, south, east, and west—are **CARDINAL DIRECTIONS**. Any point *between* two cardinal directions is an **INTERMEDIATE DIRECTION**. For example, looking north and partly to the east is said to be looking northeast. But if you turn around and glance south and partly to the west, you are looking southwest.

A **GLOBE** is the only accurate representation of our spherical Earth. Think of a globe as a scale model of Earth with a paper or plastic map mounted on its spherical surface. Globes are great to study because unlike most flat maps, they show continents and oceans in their true proportions. Size, shape, distance, and direction are all accurately represented. Projecting this round shape onto a flat sheet of paper to make a map distorts these elements. To solve the problem of distortion, mapmakers use a variety of **MAP PROJECTIONS** to portray our curved Earth on a flat sheet of paper. Each projection distorts Earth according to a mathematical calculation. Three commonly used projections are the Mercator, the Winkel Tripel, and the Goode's Interrupted Homolosine. The **MERCATOR** projection is helpful to navigators because it allows them to maintain a constant compass direction as they travel between two points, but it greatly exaggerates areas at higher latitudes. The **WINKEL TRIPEL** is a general-purpose projection popularly used for political, physical, and thematic maps because it minimizes distortion of both size and shape. The

GOODE'S INTERRUPTED HOMOLOSINE minimizes distortion of scale and shape by interrupting the globe. This type of equal-area projection is useful for mapping comparisons of various kinds of data, such as rain forests and population density.

MERCATOR

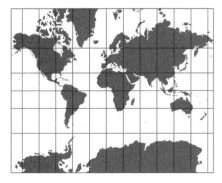

WINKEL TRIPEL

GOODE'S INTERRUPTED HOMOLOSINE

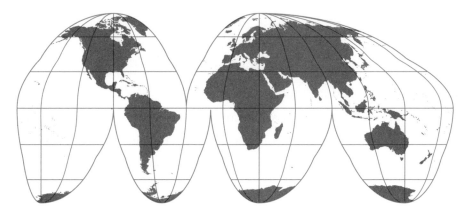

There are two main types of maps. **PHYSICAL MAPS** empha-size natural features such as mountains, rivers, lakes, deserts, and plains. Mapmakers often use shades of color to indicate different elevations. **POLITICAL MAPS** use lines to show boundaries between countries, points to show cities, and various other symbols to show roads, airports, canals, and other human-related features. Examples of these two kinds of maps are on the facing page.

We use latitude and longitude to determine the absolute loca-tion of physical and political features and **RELATIVE LOCATION** to explain the underlying reasons for that precise location and to show the interconnection of geographic phenomena.

For example, the geographic grid pinpoints Chicago's absolute location at 41°N latitude, 87°W longitude. However, the Windy City's location on the shore of Lake Michigan is *relative* to the historic water commerce routes favored by early Native Americans and settlers. Without Lake Michigan, Chicago might not exist.

Similarly, Khartoum, the capital city of Sudan, is located at 15°N latitude, 32°E longitude, *relative* to the confluence of the Blue and the White Nile. Without this confluence of rivers, this city out in the center of the Sahara would not have become such an important economic center.

Physical features are located relative to the geologic processes that created them. For example, Mount Rainier, in Washington State, is located at 47°N latitude, 122°W longitude, relative to the collision of two tectonic plates (moving slabs of Earth's crust) that created the Cascade Range. As a result, Mount Rainier shares the same geologic origin as the other volcanoes located north and

PHYSICAL MAP

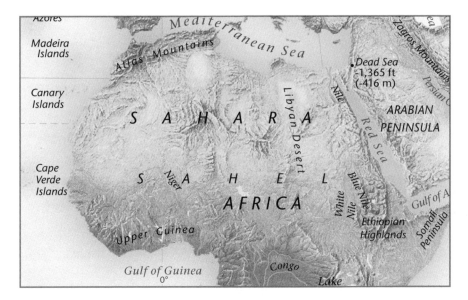

POLITICAL MAP

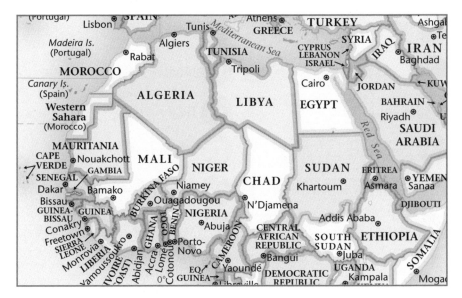

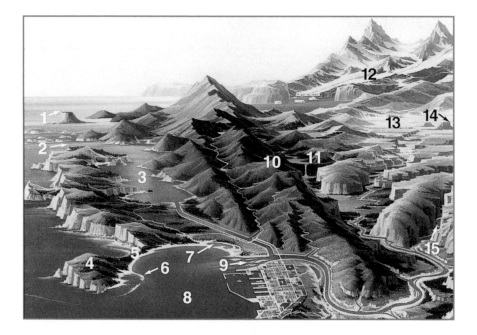

IMAGINARY LANDSCAPE

1 Volcano

2 Strait

3 Sound

4 Peninsula

5 Isthmus

6 Spit

7 Lagoon

8 Bay

9 Delta

10 Divide

11 Reservoir

12 Glacier

13 Desert

14 Mesa

15 Canyon

south of it. Without the tectonic plate boundary, this part of the Pacific Northwest would have a much different physical environment and human settlement pattern than we see today.

Use the world maps, atlases, and geographic reference books in your tool kit to learn more about these concepts and the language of maps. They are the building blocks for more learning and the source of many Bee questions.

The diagram of an imaginary landscape on the facing page was used in a round of questions in a state-level Bee to quiz students on their ability to identify physical features. Students were asked to give the number that best represented a specific physical feature. Of course, they didn't have the benefit of being able to see the answers! They are provided for you so that you can use this as a study tool for learning some very basic physical terms. You will find definitions for each of these terms in your geographical reference book. Learn them, and try to find examples of each on physical maps. You can be sure that geographic terms are a frequent topic for Bee questions.

Study the A "Bee" Cs

Once you know how to read maps, the next step is to learn the most important place-names that go on them. This memorization develops your global sense of place. Learning place-names is like learning your ABCs. Without knowing the alphabet, you can't spell words. Without knowing place-names, you can't identify places and features on a map or understand the interrelationships between physical and human activities. They are a necessary and important building block to greater geographic knowledge.

The number of place-names can be overwhelming. Organizing them into physical and political groups can be helpful. Start with the first categories in each group and work your way down. Don't just memorize a list of names and figures. Find each feature or place on the map and take time to learn about it and what it's near.

PHYSICAL FEATURES

THE CONTINENTS

	AREA		% of
	(sq mi)	(sq km)	Earth's Land
Asia	17,208,300	44,570,000	30.0
Africa	11,608,000	30,065,000	20.2
North America	9,449,000	24,474,000	16.5
South America	6,880,000	17,819,000	12.0
Antarctica	5,100,000	13,209,000	8.9
Europe	3,841,400	9,947,000	6.7
Australia	2,970,000	7,692,000	5.2

THE OCEANS

	AREA		% of Earth's
	(sq mi)	(sq km)	Water Area
Pacific	65,436,200	169,479,000	46.8
Atlantic	35,338,500	91,526,400	25.3
Indian	29,839,800	74,694,800	20.6
Arctic	5,390,000	13,960,100	3.9

Note: Although some geographers consider Europe and Asia as one continent called Eurasia, National Geographic counts them as two landmasses to make a total of seven continents. Likewise, some maps show a Southern Ocean around Antarctica. Others show this body of water as the continuation of the Atlantic, Pacific, and Indian Oceans. The tables at the bottom of the previous page list the names of the continents and oceans in order by size.

HIGHEST POINT ON EACH CONTINENT

	feet	meters
Everest, Asia	29,035	8,850
Aconcagua, S. America	22,834	6,960
McKinley (Denali), N. America	20,320	6,194
Kilimanjaro, Africa	19,340	5,895
El'brus, Europe	18,510	5,642
Vinson Massif, Antarctica	16,067	4,897
Kosciuszko, Australia	7,310	2,228

LOWEST POINT ON EACH CONTINENT

	feet	meters
Dead Sea, Asia	-1,385	-422
Lake Assal, Africa	-512	-156
Death Valley, N. America	-282	-86
Laguna del Carbón, S. America	-344	-105
Caspian Sea, Europe	-92	-28
Lake Eyre, Australia	-52	-16
Bentley Subglacial Trench, Antarctica	-8,383	-2,555

TEN LARGEST SEAS

	AREA	
	(sq mi)	(sq km)
Coral	1,615,260	4,183,510
South China	1,388,570	3,596,390
Caribbean	1.094,330	2,834,290
Bering	972,810	2,519,580
Mediterranean	953,320	2,469,100
Sea of Okhotsk	627,490	1,625,190
Gulf of Mexico	591,430	1,531,810
Norwegian	550,300	1,425,280
Greenland	447,050	1,157,850
Sea of Japan (East Sea)	389,290	1,008,260

TEN LARGEST LAKES

	AREA	
	(sq mi)	(sq km)
Caspian Sea, Europe-Asia	143,200	371,000
Superior, N. America	31,700	82,100
Victoria, Africa	26,800	69,500
Huron, N. America	23,000	59,600
Michigan, N. America	22,300	57,800
Tanganyika, Africa	12,600	32,600
Baikal, Asia	12,200	31,500
Great Bear, N. America	12,100	31,300
Malawi, Africa	11,200	28,900
Great Slave, N. America	11,000	28,600

TEN LARGEST ISLANDS

	AREA				AREA	
	(sq mi)	(sq km)			(sq mi)	(sq km)
Greenland	836,000	2,166,000	Sumatra		165,000	427,300
New Guinea	306,000	792,500	Honshu		87,800	227,400
Borneo	280,100	725,500	Great Britain		84,200	218,100
Madagascar	226,600	587,000	Victoria		83,900	217,300
Baffin	196,000	507,500	Ellesmere		75,800	196,200

LONGEST RIVERS*

	miles	kilometers
Nile, Africa	4,241	6,825
Amazon, S. America	4,000	6,437
Chang (Yangtze), Asia	3,964	6,380
Mississippi-Missouri, N. America	3,710	5,971
Murray-Darling, Australia	2,310	3,718
Volga, Europe	2,290	3,685

Antarctica has no flowing rivers

* These lists name the longest river and the major
mountain range on each continent. Rivers are listed
longest to shortest. Mountain ranges are listed in
alphabetical order.

MAJOR MOUNTAIN RANGES*

Alps, Europe

Andes, South America

Atlas Mountains, Africa

Great Dividing Range, Australia

Himalaya, Asia

Rocky Mountains, North America

Transantarctic Mountains, Antarctica

Ural Mountains form much of the boundary
between Europe and Asia

EARTH'S EXTREMES

Hottest Place: Dalol, Danakil Depression, Ethiopia;
annual average temperature—93°F (34°C)
Coldest Place: Plateau Station, Antarctica;
annual average temperature— -70.4°F (-56.7°C)
Wettest Place: Mawsynram, Assam, India;
annual average rainfall—467 in (1,187 cm)
Driest Place: Atacama Desert, Chile; rainfall
barely measurable
Highest Waterfall: Angel Falls, Venezuela;
3,212 ft (979 m)

Largest Desert: Sahara, Africa; 3,475,000 sq mi
(9,000,000 sq km)
Largest Canyon: Grand Canyon, Colorado River,
Arizona; 277 mi (446 km) long along the river;
600 ft (180 m) to 18 mi (29 km) wide; about 1.1 mi
(1.8 km) deep
Longest Reef: Great Barrier Reef, Australia;
1,429 mi (2,300 km)
Greatest Tides: Bay of Fundy, Nova Scotia,
Canada—52 ft (16 m)

THE POLITICAL WORLD

Most atlases list countries with statistical information, such as area and population, so that you can make your own chart of the largest and smallest by area and by population. Although area figures seldom change (unless there is a boundary change), population figures do. Use Web sites listed in Chapter 6 to keep up-to-date.

The countries of North America: North America is made up of 23 independent countries. It includes Canada, the United States, Mexico, the countries of Central America, the islands of the West Indies, and Greenland.

The countries of South America: South America is made up of 12 independent countries and one French territory, French Guiana.

The countries of Europe: Russia is usually counted as one of Europe's 47 independent countries. Although most of its land is in Asia, most of its people and its capital city (Moscow) are west of the Ural Mountains in Europe.

The countries of Africa: Africa has 54 independent countries. Most people live along the Nile and south of the Sahara.

The countries of Asia: China is the largest country located entirely in Asia and also the most populous of Asia's 46 countries.

Australia, New Zealand, and Oceania: Australia is a continent and a country. Geographers often include it and New Zealand with the islands of the south and central Pacific and call this region Oceania. Australia is the largest and most populous of the 14 independent countries in this region.

Antarctica: This is the only continent that has no independent countries and no permanent population.

TIP #4 Master Mental Maps

Studying geographic shapes and place-names will eventually fix mental maps in your brain. You'll be able to picture not only where a place is, but what's near it, who lives there, and lots more. The ability to produce mental images of the world characterizes all Bee champions. This requires atlas and reference book use and a good understanding of map scale.

MAP SCALE makes it possible to figure out what distance on Earth's surface is represented by a given length on a map. Large-scale maps show a limited geographic area such as a neighborhood or city in great detail. The scale on such a map may be expressed as the ratio 1:1,500, meaning that every inch on the map equals 1,500 inches on the ground. (That's 125 feet or less than half a football field.) This allows the cartographer to include street names, parks, and creeks. A large-scale map of the United States wouldn't fit in your backpack. In fact, you'd need a dump truck!

Small-scale maps have much less detail but cover a greater geographical area, such as a state, mountain range, or continent. The scale here may read 1:5,000,000 (one inch equals five million inches on the ground—a very long crawl). This level of detail is the only way to cover a large area such as a continent or the world so that you can study it as a whole.

The next step is adding more physical and cultural depth to these mental maps. The following categories will get you started.

PHYSICAL FEATURES

Vegetation Zones, or Biomes: There are four main categories of vegetation zones: forest, grassland, desert, and tundra. Start with these, then expand your knowledge by learning about the different types of vegetation within these categories. Vegetation is closely linked to climate.

Climate Zones: Climate is the long-term average weather conditions of a place. Most climate maps show at least five different zones: tropical, dry, temperate, continental, and polar. As you build your knowledge, you will become familiar with subcategories, such as tropical wet and dry, arid and semiarid, marine west coast, and Mediterranean.

CULTURAL FEATURES

Population Density: Population density is the number of people living in each square mile or kilometer of a place. The population density of a country is calculated by dividing its population by its area. Asia is the most densely populated continent; Australia is the least densely populated continent (excluding Antarctica). Check out your maps, and see if you can figure out why!

Religion: All of the world's major religions—Christianity, Hinduism, Judaism, Buddhism, Islam—as well as Shinto, Taoism, and Confucianism originated in Asia. They spread around the world as people migrated to new areas.

Languages: There are thousands of languages, but there are only 12 major language families. Languages in the Indo-European family, which includes English, Russian, and German, are spoken over the widest geographic area. Mandarin Chinese is spoken by the most people. Can you figure out why?

ECONOMIC FEATURES

World Economy: Familiarize yourself with terms such as primary, secondary, tertiary, and quaternary, as well as developed and developing, industrialized and nonindustrialized.

Commerce: Learn the major crops, minerals, and products that countries on each continent produce and export. Then take note of major trade alliances, such as NAFTA (North American Free Trade Agreement), the EU (European Union), WTO (World Trade Organization), and OPEC (Organization of Petroleum Exporting Countries).

Transportation: Study maps, charts, and graphs to learn about major trade routes by land, sea, and air.

Filling in your mental maps will take some time, so be patient. Find a study method that works for you and then hop to it!

TIP #5   **Build Your Knowledge**

Conquering place-names prepares you to tackle the biggest and most rewarding challenge of preparing for the Bee: learning about the world's primary physical and cultural patterns. Understanding how the world functions as an interconnected and dynamic system is what geography is all about. Studying these patterns prepares you to combine and layer more complex geographic information onto your basic mental maps. This takes time, but the rewards are great. The following suggestions are designed to help you reach this level.

COMBINE INFORMATION

Good geographers combine information from different sources to arrive at logical conclusions. They understand the basic patterns of climate, geology, vegetation, human settlement, migration, and commerce. Combining these patterns with a knowledge of regions and place-names will empower you to answer very specific questions that otherwise might have been a choice between two guesses. At the very least it will enable you to make an educated guess when you don't know the answer. The question analyses that follow explain how this works.

1. Which city recently suffered a severe earthquake, Tokyo or Omaha?
You may not recall any recent earthquakes, but you know that

Tokyo is in Japan, an island country off the east coast of Asia, along the tectonic Ring of Fire. Omaha is a city in Nebraska, a state located in the middle of the North American plate. Since more earthquakes occur around the rim of the Pacific Ocean than anywhere else, you correctly answer **Tokyo**.

2. Which is Germany's most important export crop, wheat or palm oil?
Using your mental maps, you know that Germany is a midlatitude country in western Europe. You also know that palm trees grow in warm tropical climates and that wheat grows in more temperate regions, like the American Midwest. Given Germany's location, you reason that it is more likely to have a temperate rather than a tropical climate, and you correctly answer **wheat**.

LEARN PATTERNS ON THE LAND

Interpreting a landscape is very different from memorizing names on a map. Geographers use **THEMATIC MAPS** to show patterns on the land. They start with a physical or a political base map and add layers of information to show whatever geographic theme they wish to emphasize—everything from world population and energy consumption *(see map opposite, top)* to shark attacks and local weather predictions.

CARTOGRAMS are special kinds of thematic maps. On them, the size of a country is based on a statistic other than land area. In the cartogram shown, population determines the size of each country. This is why Nigeria, Africa's most populous country, is shown much larger than Sudan, Africa's largest country in area.

THEMATIC MAP

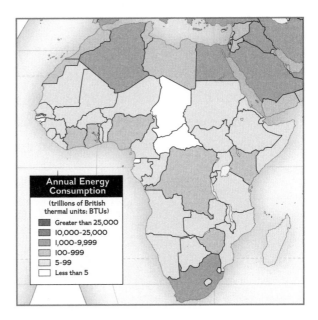

Annual Energy Consumption

(trillions of British thermal units: BTUs)

- Greater than 25,000
- 10,000–25,000
- 1,000–9,999
- 100–999
- 5–99
- Less than 5

CARTOGRAM

Morocco

Egypt

Sudan

Nigeria   Ethiopia

Uganda   Kenya

D.R.C.

Tanzania

World Population, 2010
1 block = 2 million people

Population Growth Rate
(as a percentage of total population)

- More than 3%
- 2.0 to 2.9%
- 1.0 to 1.9%
- 0 to 0.9%
- negative growth

South Africa

INTERPRETING GRAPHS

Graphs are another important tool that geographers use to convey information, and you can expect to encounter various kinds in the Bee. A special kind of bar graph called a population pyramid *(below, top)* shows the distribution of a country's population by sex and age. A more traditional style of bar graph shows water usage.

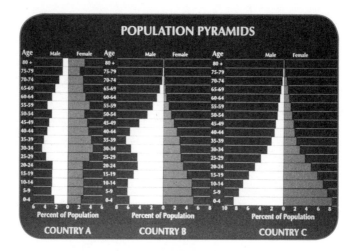

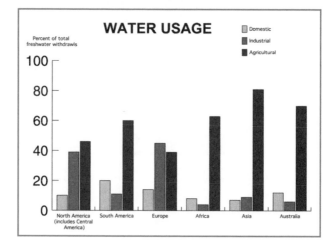

6 Make School Work for You

Geography is all around you! The first place to look is in school. History uniformly incorporates geography in discussing wars (the Russian winter froze the German Army in World War II), slavery (wind belts made the triangular trade possible), and ecological disasters (poor farming techniques and drought triggered the Dust Bowl during the 1930s). You will also find geography concepts in literature (Mark Twain, Robert Service, Laura Ingalls Wilder), science classes (especially Earth science and biology), mathematics (latitude and longitude, population studies, sun angles, etc.), and fine arts (dance, music, and paintings are all reflections of culture). You can even find geography in your school cafeteria (tacos, spaghetti, and rice). With good mental maps and the ability to combine information from different sources, you can spend your entire school day in excellent preparation for the Bee!

7 Use Your Geographic Eyes

When you can think like a geographer and understand the major patterns that influence our physical environment, culture, and economy, it's time for some field observation. The following suggestions will get your nose out of the books and into the real world.

BECOME AN OBSERVANT MALL RAT

Stores are filled with goods from every corner of the world. The origin of these products and their movement around the globe tells us much about where raw materials such as wood, minerals, and cotton come from, who makes them into finished products such as furniture, baseball bats, and shirts, and who buys them. They also furnish clues about labor use, population growth rates, and the huge difference in wealth between rich and poor countries.

Combining information from product labels and packaging with your mental maps represents advanced geographic thinking. You can practice this in stores, at school, and at home by reading the labels and packaging on products to find out where the raw materials used to make them came from and who made them.

For example, many computers are manufactured in China from European and Japanese components. They carry a U.S.A. label and are packaged in boxes made in Mexico. Most toys are manufactured in China. Much of our clothing is stitched in Mexico, Central America, or Asia. Many books are printed in

Singapore. After much practice, you will find it easier to predict which country names will appear on boxes and labels. This is great evidence that your mental maps are becoming more detailed!

Check out stores that sell furniture (look for exotic woods), electronics (identify manufactured goods with components from multiple regions), and indigenous art (that comes from everywhere). A century ago, Americans prized goods made overseas for their exotic qualities. Today, it would be extraordinarily difficult to outfit a home with products made only in North America. Global connections are the heart of the world's economy.

STOMACH MORE GEOGRAPHY

Grocery stores offer products from everywhere. Look for New Zealand kiwis, Colombian coffee, Central Asian spices, Swiss chocolate, and Mexican avocados among the zillion other products from around the world that arrive in your local food store.

Be aware that geographic place-names incorporated into product labels can sometimes lead you astray. For instance, check out fine china from Ireland, India ink bottled in South America, chili peppers grown in Mexico, English muffins baked from Nebraska wheat, and Canadian bacon from hogs raised in Iowa!

ATTEND COMMUNITY AND LOCAL EVENTS

Local communities are a great geographic resource. Keep an eye out for free concerts and lectures. Visit your museums and library display cases. If you have a college or university nearby, watch for public lectures and exhibits.

Current events questions query knowledge about natural disasters (Hurricane Katrina, fires in Greece, Andean earthquakes), cultural and political upheaval (Darfur, Myanmar, Israel and Palestine), international agreements (Kyoto Protocol, Ocean Treaty, Intellectual Piracy), and discoveries (archaeological finds, new plant species, energy, etc.). Almost any topic that is in the news, especially if it involves more than one of the categories mentioned above, is fair game for the Bee. Stories that have been the subject of recent Bee questions include the spread of AIDS, the Beijing Olympics, Iran's nuclear ambitions, and the Arab Spring.

For our purposes, we can divide current events into ongoing topics—such as global warming, immigration, and oil exploration—and breaking news stories, such as Nobel Prize announcements, international border closures, and national elections.

Your local and regional media (newspapers, TV, radio) are great ways to keep tabs on our rapidly changing world. Online news sites are also good sources, and they report events from many different perspectives. Bookmark online domestic and international newspapers so you can easily access and quickly scan them. Many of them appear in several languages, including English. They also offer great maps, photos, archived back issues, and links to related sites.

TIP
#9 **Read, Read, Read**

Bee champions share a passion for reading. They read books, magazines, newspapers, cereal boxes, Web sites—anything they can lay their eyes on. They read at school, at Grandma's, and on buses, trains, and airplanes. They read on weekends and throughout the summer. Reading helps build your mental maps of people and places around the world. At the same time, reading becomes more geographic once you have good mental maps that enliven and enrich almost any story or news item. You can add to your mental maps as you read by keeping a map handy. Use it to find new places and features and to understand relationships between the land and the people.

TIP #10 Play Games

Chapter 6 evaluates several games that use a quiz format like the Bee's to test your knowledge of geography. The Bee Web site offers geography questions to give you an idea of what the questions in the contest are like. You will find *GeoSpy, GeoBee Challenge,* and lots of other geography games at: kids.nationalgeographic.com/Games/GeographyGames

Playing these games offers several advantages. First, they simulate the Bee by asking questions from diverse topics that require an answer in a fixed amount of time. Second, they can help you identify your weak areas so that you can concentrate on improving those skills. A final advantage is that many of these games require multiple players, which doubles the opportunity to learn, promotes discussion, and lets you benefit from the knowledge of others.

There are other kinds of fun and productive study aids. Some, such as flash cards, are helpful for testing basic facts. Others are great for gathering interesting geo-tidbits. These should be treated as supplements to your learning.

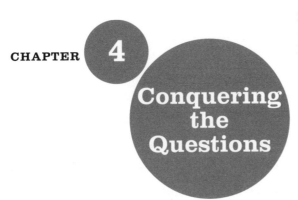

CHAPTER **4**

Conquering the Questions

Genius is one percent inspiration and ninety-nine percent perspiration.
—THOMAS ALVA EDISON

This chapter presents questions that have been used at the school, state, and national levels of the Bee. Most are from the preliminary competitions, as questions there are organized by geographic categories. Samples of map, graph, and photo questions are also included.

The objective here is not to provide questions and answers for you to memorize. Rather, it is to make you familiar with the kinds of questions asked in the Bee and show you how to look for clues within the questions that can help you come up with the right answers. Learning how to recognize the clues will reinforce the need to master the ten study tips outlined in Chapter 3. It is important to remember that the purpose of the Bee is to test your knowledge of geography. This means you don't have to worry about "trick" questions. Just take your time and think things through. Even if you answer incorrectly, you will learn something new for next time.

Before plunging into the questions, here are a few pointers to remember about the contest. First, remember the Bee is usually an oral competition (except for the written Qualifying Test that each school champion takes), so you won't have the benefit of seeing the questions in writing. It is important to listen carefully. The moderator will read each question only once, and you want to be sure to hear all the clues that might help you answer correctly.

Second, be sure to listen to the entire question before answering. Don't assume that you know what is going to be asked. You have only one chance to respond. Once you say an answer out loud, it is very unlikely that you will have time to change it before the moderator responds.

Third, don't let difficult-sounding words intimidate or sidetrack you. If the moderator trips over the pronunciation, he or she should automatically repeat the entire question. If you think having a word spelled will help you, then ask the moderator to spell it out. Just be aware that you can interrupt the competition only two times to ask either to have a question repeated or a word spelled. This rule applies to the Preliminary Competition and to the Final Round at each level of the Bee.

Finally, always speak very clearly with your best pronunciation. Don't worry if microphones are present, because they make you sound very cool and extra important!

Some Bee rounds involve questions from a single topic, such as cultural geography; others are a mix of many topics. The first few rounds usually offer a choice of two answers so that you have a 50-50 chance of answering correctly. This is to help you relax. Gradually, the questions become more difficult as you progress from round to round and from one level to the next. After all, the Bee is a contest, and ultimately only one student can be the champion. But if you stay cool, use your study tips, and look for clues, you'll be surprised at how many questions you will be able to answer correctly.

The questions that follow are organized first by the level of the Bee in which they were used, and then by the round in which they appeared. Since the titles of rounds can change from year to year, and since the sample questions are taken from several different years, the titles listed here are only representative of what you might encounter. You may also notice that some questions could fit in more than one category. This overlap is just the nature of geography. The round titles will give you a general idea of the focus of the questions included in them. The first question in each round is followed by a discussion in italics that points out clues and reminds you of the study tips that will lead you to the correct answer (in bold type). For the remaining questions in the round you are on your own. You will find the answers starting on page 123.

As you go through the questions, jot down new terms, facts, and place-names. Keep your study tools handy so you can put questions in their geographic context. Try timing yourself to get practice in answering within the 15-second time limit (12 seconds for the national Final Round questions). Since the Bee is usually an oral competition, consider having someone read the questions to you. That will teach you to listen carefully for clues. Most of all, have fun!

SCHOOL-LEVEL PRELIMINARY ROUNDS

Round 1: U.S. Geography

1. Which state has areas that are prone to avalanches—Colorado or Kansas?

*The word "avalanches" is the clue here. From studying geographic terms, you know they are moving masses of snow that occur in high mountains. From your physical maps you know that Colorado has lots of mountains, so you correctly answer **Colorado.***

2. The York River empties into the Chesapeake Bay from which state—Virginia or Massachusetts?

3. Native American tribes living on the prairie were prominent in the history of which state—Illinois or Alaska?

4. Which state has a coastline on the Gulf of Mexico—Alabama or Delaware?

5. Which state is closer to the Continental, or Great, Divide—North Carolina or Idaho?

6. Which state has a longer border with Canada—North Dakota or New Hampshire?

7. Which state is located farther north—Maryland or New Mexico?

8. Which state has a higher average elevation—Louisiana or Colorado?

9. The Colorado River flows through which state—Arizona or New Jersey?

10. The Appalachian Mountains cover much of which state—Pennsylvania or Kansas?

11. Which state has a smaller area—Delaware or South Dakota?

12. Which state is farther east—Nebraska or South Carolina?

Round 2: U. S. Cities

1. Which city is located just north of the aquatic Biscayne National Park—Minot, North Dakota, or Miami, Florida?
The clue "aquatic" is the key here. Water surrounds much of Florida, which is also famous for swamps, so you eliminate landlocked North Dakota. Many Bee questions refer to national parks throughout the United States, so from studying the names and locations of parks, you correctly answer **Miami, Florida.**

2. Which city is located along the Erie Canal—Syracuse, New York, or Pittsburgh, Pennsylvania?

3. Which city is located closer to the Tropic of Cancer—Sacramento, California, or San Antonio, Texas?

4. Which city is located on the eastern side of the Cascade Range—Eureka, California, or Spokane, Washington?

5. Which city is located in the heavily agricultural San Joaquin [wahkeen] Valley— Phoenix, Arizona, or Fresno, California?

6. Which city is located in the Blue Ridge Mountains—Asheville, North Carolina, or Williamsburg, Virginia?

7. Which city is more at risk of being hit by tropical storms—San Juan, Puerto Rico, or Roswell, New Mexico?

8. Which city is located just northwest of the Hoover Dam—Las Vegas, Nevada, or Pueblo, Colorado?

9. Which city is located in a region where dairy farming is a major activity—Green Bay, Wisconsin, or Cheyenne, Wyoming?

10. Which city is located just inland from a chain of barrier islands known as the Sea Islands—Savannah, Georgia, or Huntington, West Virginia?

11. Which city lies on the Ozark Plateau—Shreveport, Louisiana, or Springfield, Missouri?

12. Which city is located immediately east of Pikes Peak—Colorado Springs, Colorado, or Boise, Idaho?

Round 3: Odd Item Out

1. Which country does *not* border the Atlantic Ocean—Mauritania, Cameroon, or Tanzania?
Drawing on your mental map of Africa, you know that the Atlantic Ocean borders the west coast where Mauritania and Cameroon are located, while the Indian Ocean borders the east coast where Tanzania is. So, you correctly answer **Tanzania.**

2. Which state does *not* have a coastline on Delaware Bay—Virginia, Delaware, or New Jersey?

3. Which present-day state is *not* located on land that was part of the Louisiana Purchase in 1803—Arkansas, Ohio, or Missouri?

4. Which state is *not* located in a humid temperate climate zone—Georgia, Vermont, or Mississippi?

5. Which state is *not* located in the mountain time zone—Kentucky, Colorado, or Montana?

6. Which state does *not* have a city of over a million people—Illinois, Pennsylvania, or Idaho?

7. Which state does *not* share a border with the Canadian province of Saskatchewan—Montana, Maine, or North Dakota?

8. Which state does *not* border the Gulf of Mexico—South Carolina, Mississippi, or Alabama?

9. Which present-day state was *not* part of the route of Lewis and Clark—Missouri, Washington, or Oklahoma?

10. Which state does *not* have a capital city located in the Rocky Mountains—Montana, Colorado, or Oregon?

11. Which state does *not* have an international border—Texas, New Hampshire, or Mississippi?

12. Which state did *not* experience a large growth in population from 2000 to 2005—North Dakota, Arizona, or Nevada?

Round 4: Continents

1. Scientists believe that about 120 million years ago, South America began to break away from which other continent?
*From learning about plate tectonics and from studying the shapes of continents and their positions in relationship to one another, you correctly answer **Africa**.*

2. Water being diverted for irrigation has caused the Aral Sea to shrink. The sea is located on which continent?

3. The Gulf of Carpentaria, located east of the city of Darwin, creates a wide indent in the coast of which continent?

4. The Estonian Orthodox Church was organized in a northern region of which continent?

5. The lowest recorded temperature in the world occurred east of the Ross Sea on which continent?

6. Asunción [ah-soon-seeohn] and Sucre [soo-kray] are capital cities located south of the Equator on which continent?

7. Buddhism is practiced by the majority of the population in over half a dozen countries on which continent?

8. The Gulf Stream is an ocean current that flows north along the eastern coast of which continent?

9. The Tropic of Cancer crosses through large deserts and Lake Nasser in the northern part of which continent?

10. The potato and the tomato both originated in the Andean highlands of which continent?

11. Queensland and New South Wales are political units located on the smallest continent. Name this continent.

12. Despite its isolated location in the Atlantic Ocean, Iceland is considered to be a part of which continent located to its east?

Round 5: Physical Geography

1. What is the term for part of an ocean or sea that cuts far into the bordering landmass and may contain one or more bays?

From studying physical features on maps and using your geographical reference book, you narrow your choices to two terms: bay and gulf. Since the word "bay" is used in the question, you eliminate it as a possibility and correctly answer **gulf.**

2. Which is the term for the vertical distance from sea level to a point on Earth's surface—elevation or latitude?

3. Which feature is formed when soil, rock, and other material are deposited by a glacier—moraine or dune?

4. Which phenomenon can be generated by an undersea earthquake—tsunami or hurricane?

5. Which is the term for the layer of Earth between the core and the crust—mantle or magma?

6. Which feature consists of a group of islands—peninsula or archipelago?

7. Which is the term for the leafy layer of treetops in a forest—rain shadow or canopy?

8. Which is the term for a long, deep depression on the ocean floor—trench or island?

9. Which metal is a main component of the super-heated core inside Earth—iron or copper?

10. Which is the term for the location where a river enters a larger body of water, such as a lake or an ocean—channel or mouth?

11. Which is the term for the flowing movement of water in one direction in an ocean orriver—current or typhoon?

12. Which landform is a tall, steep-sided tower of rock that eroded from a mesa—canyon or butte?

Round 6: Fresh Water

1. More than 80 million people use the Danube River for drinking water, irrigation, industry, and other activities as it winds its way east through Europe. The river's mouth is in which country—Spain or Romania?

*If you recall the physical world map, specifically the longest rivers of the world (under Tip #3: Study the A "Bee" Cs), you will correctly answer **Romania**. More advanced geographers will also visualize how the Pyrenees Mountains separate Spain—and its rivers—from the rest of Europe.*

2. The Rio de la Plata is a source of drinking water and forms part of the border between Uruguay and which other country—Argentina or Venezuela?

3. The Great Man-Made River project taps water from beneath the Sahara in which country—Turkey or Libya?

4. A reservoir at Angat Dam provides water to Manila in which country—Philippines or New Zealand?

5. People in Santo Domingo are encouraged to drink bottled water because clean water sources are scarce. This city is located in which Caribbean country—Dominican Republic or Jamaica?

6. Desalination of salt water from the Persian Gulf provides fresh water to people in which country—Saudi Arabia or Tunisia?

7. The Coppermine River, which is used for fishing but is difficult to navigate due to many rapids, has its source north of Great Slave Lake in which country—Canada or Norway?

8. The Godavari [go-dah-vuh-ree] River, which rises in Maharashtra [mah-huh-rahsh-truh] state, is a sacred waterway to Hindus in which country—India or Afghanistan?

9. Before entering the Aegean Sea, the Piniós [pee-nyohs] River is a location for tourist activities in Thessaly, a region in which country—Greece or Slovenia?

10. The Limpopo River serves as a border for multiple African countries before it empties into the Indian Ocean on the coast of which country—Cameroon or Mozambique?

Round 7: Cultural Geography

1. Spices such as cinnamon, cumin, chili, and turmeric have been used not only as flavoring but also as medicine in South Asia's largest country. Name this country.

From studying political regions in your atlases, you know that South Asia is usually considered to include India, Pakistan, Bangladesh, Nepal, and Bhutan. A quick check of your mental map tells you which is the largest, so you correctly answer **India.**

2. The Hagia Sophia was built during the 6th century A.D. in Constantinople. This building still stands today and is located in which present-day country?

3. About one-third of the population of a North American country is of either English or French ethnic descent. Name this country.

4. After a long legal battle, the Maori were granted legal rights to a traditional war chant in which country?

5. The lungi [loon-ghee] is a traditional garment worn by men in many South Asian countries, including the region's largest. Name this country.

6. The Basilica of Guadalupe celebrates the patroness of a country whose population is over 75 percent Roman Catholic. Name this North American country.

7. Kiswahili [kih-swah-hee-lee] and English are the official languages of an African country that borders Lake Victoria and Lake Turkana. Name this country.

8. People still read legendary tales written in Old Norse prose called sagas because their present-day language is so similar in which European island country?

9. The population of the world's fourth largest island is made up of about 20 different ethnic groups. Name this island country located off the coast of Africa.

10. Shifting political boundaries after World War I resulted in a loss of population for a country that had been part of an empire with Austria. Name this present-day landlocked country that is divided by the Danube River.

Tiebreaker Questions

1. The Tropic of Capricorn passes through the largest island in the Indian Ocean. Name this island.

You know from studying lines of latitude that the Tropic of Capricorn is 23$^{1}/_{2}$° south of the Equator. From your mental maps you know that the Indian Ocean lies between Africa and Australia. Running down your list of the world's ten largest islands, you correctly answer **Madagascar.**

2. Which U.S. territory is the largest and the southernmost of the Mariana Islands?

3. Johannesburg is located on the High Veld, a broad, grassy plain in what country?

4. What term describes a narrow strip of land that connects two larger landmasses?

5. The Dnieper [nee-pur] River flows through Kiev before emptying into what sea?

6. The island of Zealand, which is located near the entrance to the Baltic Sea, is part of what country?

7. Central America's largest lake shares its name with a country. Name this lake.

8. A strait named for an explorer separates the mainland of South America from Tierra del Fuego. Name this strait.

SCHOOL-LEVEL FINAL ROUND

The questions in the Final Round are similar to those in the Preliminary Competition, except they are more difficult. The questions are not grouped into geographic categories. Instead, it is a good bet that each question will test your knowledge about a different geographic subject. The exception to this is the series of questions that pertains to a map, graph, or other visual aid.

Map Questions

To answer the questions below, you will have to use the map showing longitude and latitude on the facing page. This round tests your ability to identify U.S. states from their shapes. During the Bee you will be given 15 seconds to study the map before answering your question.

1. The coordinates 45°N latitude, 90°W longitude intersect in what state?

2. The southern border of what state aligns with 35°N latitude?

3. The southern tip of what state crosses 25°N latitude?

4. Part of the western border of what state aligns with 120°W latitude?

5. If you were to travel east from Utah along 40°N latitude, what state would you cross first?

6. The coordinates 40°N latitude, 80°W longitude intersect close to the southwest border of what state?

7. The coordinates 35°N latitude, 80°W longitude intersect in what state?

8. If you were to travel south from Minnesota along 95°W longitude, what state would you cross first?

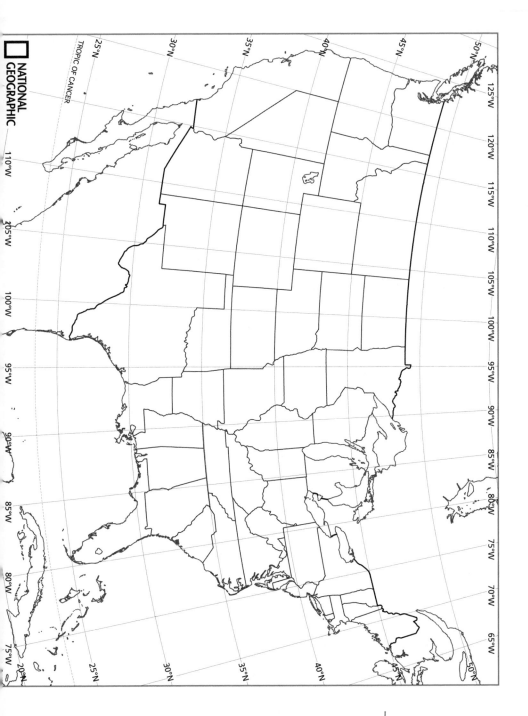

NATIONAL
GEOGRAPHIC

TROPIC OF CANCER

25°N

25°N

30°N

35°N

40°N

45°N

50°N

30°N

35°N

40°N

45°N

20°N

125°W

120°W

115°W

110°W

105°W

100°W

95°W

90°W

85°W

80°W

75°W

70°W

65°W

110°W

105°W

100°W

95°W

90°W

85°W

80°W

75°W

QUALIFYING TEST

The Qualifying Test is the only part of the Bee that is completely written. The 70 questions, including a set pertaining to a map, graph, or other visual aid, cover a wide variety of geographic topics. Each question offers a choice of four answers, and you must choose the number (1, 2, 3, or 4) that you believe identifies the correct answer. Remember, the only time that you will take this test is if you are the winner of your School Bee.

1. The Olmec, one of Middle America's first civilizations, lived in a region bordering which body of water?

Gulf of California	1
Gulf of Mexico	2
Caribbean Sea	3
Chesapeake Bay	4

The Middle America clue eliminates Chesapeake Bay. You know that some of the earliest civilizations were in southern Mexico, so you correctly answer **2.**

2. Where do all lines of longitude meet?

Arctic Circle	1
Tropic of Capricorn	2
Equator	3
North and South Poles	4

3. The term rust belt is used for the region south of the Great Lakes that was historically important for which activity?

fishing	1
manufacturing	2
mining	3
logging	4

4. Which of the following was most responsible for the spread of the English language to many regions during the 19th century?

British colonialism	1
Christian missionaries	2
Internet communication	3
American popular culture	4

5. Which of the following provides the signals that global positioning system (GPS) receivers use to determine a location on Earth's surface?

International Space Station	1
Greenwich Observatory	2
geographic information systems (GIS)	3
satellites	4

6. Which type of cloud is thin and wispy and found at high altitudes?

cirrus	1
cumulus	2
stratus	3
cumulonimbus	4

7. Which is a characteristic of the Amazon River that makes its waters visibly different from the ocean waters at the river's mouth?

It is polluted by industrial chemicals	1
It carries a large amount of silt	2
Its water is warmer than seawater	3
It carries fresh water, not salt water	4

8. Which event occurs when the moon passes between Earth and the sun and appears to block all or part of the sun's rays?

equinox	1
eclipse	2
solstice	3
inversion	4

9. If a developing country improved its health care and sanitation systems, which direct result would be expected?

longer life expectancy	1
higher death rate	2
higher fertility rate	3
lower population growth rate	4

Analogies

The Qualifying Test almost always has a series of analogies in which you are asked to compare two things that have something in common. For example, in the analogy "The peso is to Mexico as the WHAT is to Japan?" the answer is yen because yen is the currency of Japan, just as the peso is the currency in Mexico. See if you can figure out the following analogies.

10. A pilgrimage to Mecca is to Muslims as bathing in the Ganges River is to WHOM?

Buddhists	1
Christians	2
Hindus	3
Jews	4

11. The Sonoran Desert is to the saguaro cactus as WHAT is to the giant sequoia tree?

Appalachian Mountains	1
Great Plains	2
Gulf Coast	3
Sierra Nevada	4

12. The Pyramids at Giza are to Egypt as the pyramids at Chichén Itzá are to WHAT?

Greece	1
Italy	2
Laos	3
Mexico	4

Map Questions

Use the weather map (opposite page) to answer these questions.

13. Which state has temperatures in the 90s?

North Dakota	1
Texas	2
California	3
South Carolina	4

14. Which of the following is the major factor in the weather of Montana?

high pressure	1
low pressure	2
cold front	3
stationary front	4

15. Which of the following cities would be more likely to experience flash flooding?

Seattle	1
Little Rock	2
Louisville	3
Richmond	4

16. Over which state are there two air masses separated by a stationary front?

Utah	1
Oklahoma	2
Oregon	3
Tennessee	4

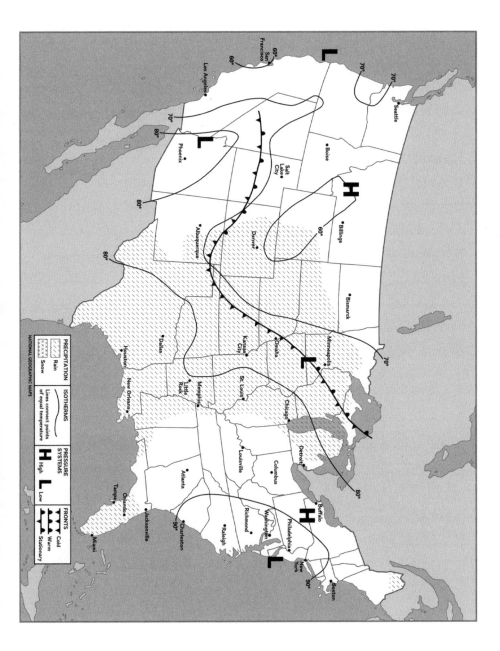

STATE-LEVEL PRELIMINARY ROUNDS

At the state level, before the official questioning begins, there is a warm-up round to help you relax. Your answers to these questions do not count. As with the school level, the first few rounds at the state level offer a choice of answers.

Round 1: U.S. Geography

1. Which state has a panhandle—Florida OR Tennessee?
Here you must rely on your mental map of the world. Avid readers will remember reading about the Florida Panhandle—not the Tennessee Panhandle—since it doesn't exist. You correctly answer **Florida.**

2. Which state has more acreage dedicated to agriculture— Nebraska OR Massachusetts?

3. Which state has more coal reserves—Florida OR Kentucky?

4. Which state extends farther north—New Hampshire OR Connecticut?

5. Which state produces more rice—California OR Vermont?

6. Which state produces more iron ore—Minnesota OR Florida?

7. The geographical center of the United States is in which

state—Texas OR South Dakota?

8. Which state is dominated by mountains in its west and plains in its east—Florida OR Colorado?

9. Which state is located west of the Great Plains—Arizona OR Iowa?

10. Which state is more mountainous—Indiana OR Alaska?

11. Which state receives more annual precipitation on average—Maryland OR North Dakota?

12. Which state contains more Civil War battlefields—North Carolina OR South Dakota?

Round 2: Physical Geography

1. Which term describes a body of water that occasionally or seasonally dries up—intermittent or brackish?
*The words "occasionally" and "seasonally" suggest not continuous, so you correctly answer **intermittent.***

2. The harmattan [har-muh-tan], which originates in the Sahara and blows over western Africa, is an example of which kind of wind—seasonal OR downdraft?

3. Which of the following is a term used to describe a dried-up lake bed in a desert basin—playa OR polder?

4. What is the term for a large structure formed when volcanic material does not flow easily and piles up around the structure's vent—sill OR lava dome?

5. Which term describes a semi-arid region dominated by grasses and shrubs—steppe OR taiga?

6. Which term refers to a sharp-crested mountain ridge formed through glacial erosion—arête [uh-rate] OR moraine

7. Which source of renewable energy can be accessed by digging deep wells to utilize hot water and steam from underground—biomass OR geothermal?

8. Which feature is built into a dam to allow migratory fish like salmon to swim upstream—ladder OR spillway?

9. Which wind phenomenon exists at both subtropical and polar latitudes—jet stream OR hurricane?

10. Which term is used to describe an area where brown algae houses a wide diversity of marine life—cold seep OR kelp forest?

Round 3: Odd Item Out

1. Which country is *not* part of the Southern Cone region in South America—Argentina, Chile, or Ecuador?
Using your mental map of South America, you know that Chile and Argentina are neighboring countries that extend to the southern tip of South America. Ecuador, on the other hand, straddles the Equator in the northern part of the continent. You conclude that the correct answer is **Ecuador**.

2. Which river does *not* flow predominantly north—the Mackenzie River, the Volga River, or the Nile River?

3. Which country's currency is *not* called the dollar—Australia, El Salvador, or Malaysia?

4. Which city is *not* a capital of one of the United Kingdom's political units—Cardiff, Belfast, or Canterbury?

5. Which island is *not* an overseas territory of France— Guadeloupe, Tahiti, or Bermuda?

6. Which city is *not* a major financial center—Hong Kong, London, or Venice?

7. On which continent would you *not* find bears in the wild— Europe, Asia, or Africa?

8. Which city is *not* the most populous in its country—Dakar, Budapest, or Bangalore?

9. Penguins are *not* indigenous to which continent—South America, Antarctica, or Asia?

10. Which country is *not* a member of the Commonwealth of Nations—United Kingdom, Australia, or Saudi Arabia?

11. Which sea is *not* adjacent to the African coastline—the Mediterranean Sea, the Andaman Sea, or the Red Sea?

12. Which country's population does *not* include a large percentage of Hindus—Cambodia, India, or Nepal?

Round 4: Economic Geography

1. Which Canadian province produces more than half of the country's manufactured goods?
You know from your mental maps that Ontario borders all of the Great Lakes and has access to the St. Lawrence Seaway. This puts it in a better position than any other Canadian province to import materials needed for manufacturing and to export finished goods. So you correctly answer **Ontario.**

2. Sugarcane is grown for export in the lowlands south of Quetzaltenango [ket-sahl-tay-nahn-go], in which country that borders El Salvador?

3. Rubber is among the exports of a country that lies east of Laos and is west of the Chinese island of Hainan. Name this country.

4. An East African country that straddles the Equator and borders the Indian Ocean is known for its exports of coffee, tea, and flowers. Name this country.

5. The world's largest landlocked country produces a significant amount of uranium. Name this country west of Mongolia.

6. Dobruja [do-broo-jah], an agricultural region known for sunflower production, includes areas along the Black Sea in Romania and what neighboring country to the south?

7. The world's largest dairy export company has its headquarters in which island country south of Fiji?

8. The port city of Boma, near the Atlantic Ocean, exports timber and bananas from what country that borders Angola?

9. Mining of phosphates has been a major industry in Jordan and is now a growing industry in what neighboring country to the north?

10. Diving for sponges is a significant industry in the Dodecanese [doh-deh-kuh-nees] Islands in the eastern Aegean Sea. These islands are part of which European Union member country?

Round 5: Current Events

The questions in this round assume that you are keeping up with events in the news. If you are, then chances are, coming up with the answers will be easy. Just in case you aren't, you'll find location clues that will help you arrive at the correct answer.

1. In September 2010, construction began on a railway extension between the cities of Lhasa [la-suh] and Xigaze [she-gah-dzuh] in which country—Bangladesh OR China?

2. In September 2010, Julia Gillard attended the opening of Parliament as her country's first female prime minister. That event took place in the capital territory northeast of Melbourne in which country—Australia OR Sweden?

3. In August 2010, reports were released about the discovery of Neanderthal sleeping chambers in Cantabria. This province is in the northern part of the Iberian Peninsula in which country—Switzerland OR Spain?

4. In the fall of 2010, construction was under way on a city called Masdar, which was designed to be sustainable in a desert environment. This city is being built near Abu Dhabi in which country—Jordan OR United Arab Emirates?

5. In September 2010, reports were released about the discovery of the Mount Nimba reed frog, which had been thought to be extinct.

The Nimba Mountains are located where Côte d'Ivoire borders Liberia and which other country—Guinea OR Cameroon?

6. In September 2010, a nighttime Formula One auto race in a city just south of the Malay Peninsula was expected to increase tourism for which country—Laos OR Singapore?

7. In October 2010, toxic red sludge flowed from a broken storage reservoir and flooded villages in an area east of the Austrian border in which country—Hungary OR Bulgaria?

8. In October 2010, it was reported that digital copies of the Dead Sea Scrolls would be made available on the Internet. The scrolls were found in the mid-1900s south of Lebanon in which country—Israel OR Kyrgyzstan?

9. In the fall of 2010, Kim Jong Un took a more prominent role in the leadership of a communist country bordering China. This led to speculation that he would succeed his father as leader of which country—North Korea OR Cambodia?

10. In October 2010, cuts to government funding of higher education affected universities, including those in Cambridge and Cardiff. These cities are in which country—Portugal OR United Kingdom?

Round 6: U.S. Species in Danger

1. Loss of native grasslands is a threat to the San Joaquin kit fox in which state—Rhode Island or California?

*Although you might not recognize this fox, select **California** because the San Joaquin Valley is a major geographic feature that appears on the maps of the Golden State. But remember, you can't always trust a fox, or any other plant or animal with a place-name attached to it. For example, the Rocky Mountain bighorn sheep range from British Columbia to Arizona. If you don't know an answer, however, this strategy will work most of the time.*

2. A national wildlife refuge provides protection for Key deer in a wetland area on Big Pine Key in which state—Florida OR Arizona?

3. The Karner blue butterfly is responding to a conservation plan to protect its habitat near the Great Lakes in which state—Wisconsin OR West Virginia?

4. The endangered nehe [nay-hay] plant's range includes Kahoolawe [kah-ho-oh-lah-way] Island, where efforts are under way to restore indigenous vegetation. This island is in which state—Hawaii OR New Jersey?

5. Jesup's milk-vetch, a rare plant related to peas, grows along a roughly 15-mile stretch of the Connecticut River in which state—Ohio OR Vermont?

6. Pesticides that are washed into the Susquehanna River are a danger to one type of darter fish in which state—Maryland OR Utah?

7. Endangered West Indian manatees seeking shallow water and sea grass can often be found in the waters near Mobile Bay in which state—Delaware OR Alabama?

8. Snake River physa [fy-suh] snails, which need cool, flowing water, are decreasing in number in which state—Idaho OR Virginia?

9. In an effort to get them to nest in an urban environment, captive-bred peregrine falcons have been released from the tops of buildings in Omaha in which state—Nebraska OR Maine?

10. The loss of prairie dogs as a food source is one reason the number of black-footed ferrets has decreased in areas near the Missouri River in which state—North Dakota OR New York?

Round 7: World Geography

1. Which country is on a peninsula—Czech Republic or Portugal? *A quick check of your mental map of Europe reveals that the Czech Republic is landlocked, so the correct answer is* **Portugal.**

2. Which country includes part of the Sahara—Algeria OR Zimbabwe?

3. Which country has a landscape that has been altered by continental glaciers—Malaysia OR Canada?

4. Which country is north of the Amazon Basin—Bolivia OR Venezuela?

5. Which country is more populous—Nigeria OR Senegal?

6. Which country experiences more earthquakes—Afghanistan OR Angola?

7. Which country is in the Alps mountain system—Slovenia OR Sweden?

8. Which country has a larger urban population—Argentina OR Guatemala?

9. Which country borders the Persian Gulf—Yemen OR Qatar?

10. Which country is landlocked—Nepal OR Cambodia?

Tiebreaker Questions

1. Name the country that controls the straits that connect the Mediterranean and Black Seas.
From your mental physical maps you know that these straits are at the eastern end of the Mediterranean Sea. Your mental political map of the region shows you that only one country borders

both the Black Sea and the Mediterranean Sea. Reasoning that this country would control the straits, you correctly answer **Turkey.**

2. The European Food Safety Authority is located in the city of Parma in what country?

3. The 2010 World Cup final was held at Soccer City Stadium in the most populous city in South Africa. Name this city.

4. James Bay, which borders Ontario and Quebec, is a southern extension of what inland body of water?

5. A highway that was constructed in the 1960s connects Phuntsholing [pin-sol-ing],near the Indian border, with the capital city of Thimphu. This highway is in which Himalayan country?

6. Although Amsterdam is the constitutional capital of the Netherlands, the country's seat of government is in what city on the North Sea?

7. The cities of Campinas, Fortaleza, and Recife each have more than one million residents in which Portuguese-speaking country?

8. The Ruwenzori Mountains, which include Margherita Peak, are on the western border of what country?

STATE-LEVEL FINAL ROUND

The only rounds of questions organized by topics in the State Finals are those that deal with a theme or visual materials, such as maps, graphs, or photographs. The following randomly selected examples are designed to give you an idea of what you can expect for these kinds of rounds.

Oral Analogies

This series of questions requires you to complete an analogy by providing the missing element. Here is an example of an analogy: Mount McKinley is to North America as Mount Everest is to WHAT? Mount McKinley is the highest peak on the continent of North America, and Mount Everest is the highest peak in Asia, so the answer is Asia.

1. The Green Mountains are to Vermont as the Brooks Range is to WHAT?

2. The Potomac River is to the Appalachian Mountains as the San Joaquin River is to WHAT?

3. Omaha is to the Missouri River as Fargo is to WHAT?

4. Granite Peak is to Montana as Guadalupe Peak is to WHAT?

5. Green Bay is to Lake Michigan as Saginaw Bay is to WHAT?

6. Puget Sound is to Washington as Suwannee Sound is to WHAT?

7. Sky Harbor International Airport is to Phoenix as John F. Kennedy International Airport is to WHAT?

8. The Battle of Antietam is to Maryland as the Battle of Shiloh is to WHAT?

9. Los Angeles is to the San Gabriel Mountains as Salt Lake City is to WHAT?

10. Arches National Park is to the Colorado River as Big Bend National Park is to WHAT?

11. The Arkansas River is to the Mississippi River as the Tennessee River is to WHAT?

Photo Questions

1. The Battle of Valcour Bay, which took place on Lake Champlain in 1776, delayed the British invasion of the Hudson Valley. Lake Champlain is located on the western side of what state?

2. The West Thumb Geyser Basin is located on the edge of Yellowstone Lake. This area of high geothermal activity is located in what state?

3. Lake of the Ozarks is impounded by Bagnell Dam and provides electricity and recreational opportunities in what state located north of Arkansas?

4. Crater Lake, formed in the caldera of a collapsed volcano, has no inlet or outlet and is located in the southern half of the Cascade Range in what state?

Map Questions

To answer the questions in this series, you will need figure out which landmark is misplaced by referring to the maps accompanying each question. During the Bee you will be given 15 seconds to study the map and give your answer.

1. On this map, which landmark has been placed in the wrong state—Great Smoky Mountains National Park, Big Bend National Park, or Everglades National Park?

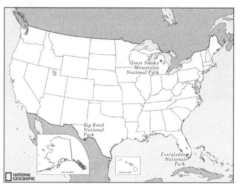

2. On this map, which landmark has been placed in the wrong state—Glacier National Park, Bunker Hill Monument, or Statue of Liberty National Monument?

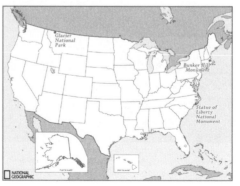

3. On this map, which landmark has been placed in the wrong state—Golden Gate National Recreation Area, Craters of the Moon National Monument and Preserve, or Carlsbad Caverns National Park?

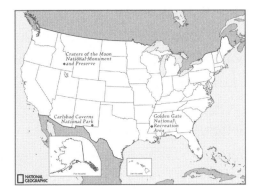

4. On this map, which landmark has been placed in the wrong state—Mount Rushmore National Memorial, Martin Luther King, Jr. National Historic Site, or Motor Cities National Heritage Area?

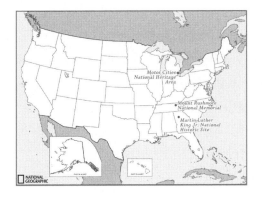

NATIONAL-LEVEL PRELIMINARY ROUNDS

The following questions are representative of the questions and geographic categories in the National Preliminary Competition.

Round 1: Paths of Explorers

1. Which explorer shares his name with the river he followed north to its mouth on the Beaufort Sea—Alexander Mackenzie OR Pierre-Esprit Radisson [pe-ehr-es-PREE rah-dee-SOHN]?

2. To test a hypothesis that the original inhabitants of Polynesian islands sailed there from South America, which explorer sailed on a raft called the Kon-Tiki—Thor Heyerdahl OR Vitus Bering?

Round 2: Alternative Energy

1. Geothermal energy from volcanic activity in the Great Rift Valley near Lake Turkana is used to generate electricity. Most of Lake Turkana is in what country?

2. Government tax incentives encourage renewable energy projects in a country where volcanoes on some of its several thousand islands are a potential source of geothermal energy. Name this country that borders the Indian Ocean.

Round 3: Cultural Geography

1. Bhangra [bahn-grah], a type of popular dance music that combines folk traditions with Western pop music, originated in

the Punjab region that straddles the border between India and which other Asian country?

2. Casas de la Trova are government cultural centers where live performances preserve and celebrate a country's musical heritage. These centers are found in several cities west of Guantánamo [gwahn-tah-nah-mo] Province in which Caribbean country?

Round 4: World Festivals
1. The annual summer solstice festival, Las Hogueras de San Juan, is celebrated with bonfires, music, and food in the coastal city of Alicante. This city is located southwest of the Balearic Islands in which European country?

2. Junkanoo, a festival of parades with elaborate costumes, music, and dances, is held on Boxing Day and New Year's Day in an island country located northwest of the Turks and Caicos Islands. Name this country.

Round 5: Physical Geography
1. Which physical feature would be considered part of the cryosphere portion of Earth's hydrosphere—ice shelf or lagoon?

2. Which type of rock has fine grains and makes up most of the oceanic crust—basalt or granite?

CHAPTER **5**

Tips From Bee Finalists

I now think almost anything is possible if I work hard enough.
—NICHOLAS JACHOWSKI
HAWAII STATE BEE
CHAMPION, 2001

This chapter provides advice from school, state, and national champions about when to get involved, what to study, and how to relax. Although some of the contributors are now in high school, at one time or another they were all Bee kids just like you. So listen up!

• •

Always study with an atlas nearby. If you encounter a place that you haven't heard of, you can look it up in the atlas's index. In addition, just looking at maps in an atlas will help you visualize the relative position of two places—a skill that is very important, since many Bee questions contain directions (north of, southeast of, and so on) that can help you "locate" the answer. You should also find somebody who will help you study, whether a coach, parent, sibling, friend or some combination of them. They can quiz you and keep you motivated. You will remember more when you study for the Bee with someone else rather than learning alone.

The Bee is a great experience—take somebody else along for the ride!
Tine Valencic, 2010, 2011 State Bee Champion, Texas (6th-7th grades); 2011 National Champion (7th grade)

●●●●●●●●●●●●●●●●●●●●●●●●●●

Planning is everything. Without planning, you can't go anywhere. Here is what I did: I set up a fixed timetable to allocate at least one hour a day during the week for geography and a little more time on the weekends. I would follow the timetable religiously. This ensured that I dedicated time for geography. Furthermore, one day I would study rivers, the next day, lakes, the following day, islands, and so on. This enabled reiteration and variation and therefore was not boring. I also learned all the surrounding facts about a location—not just the abstract data. For example, when learning about the Great Lakes, identify and learn all of the cities on their shores, the area, industries, and any sources of water that flow into the lakes, then connect the dots. One trick that helped me was to collect twenty new facts a day. Doing so helped me to learn more than 100 new facts a week! Finally, don't panic and never give up. I missed the very first question in the national finals on TV, but I did not give up and made it through the whole competition by keeping myself calm and cool. Now that you have taken the first step by purchasing this great book, best of luck for a great Geo journey!
Aadith Moorthy, 2010 State Bee Champion, Florida (8th Grade); 2010 National Champion (8th Grade)

••••••••••••••••••••••••••

Don't be overwhelmed by all the things you need to know. Tackle geography step by step. Just about anything can pop up in a Bee question, but I would recommend starting with the most important and essential information first: the continents, countries, and capitals, then move on to their major physical features, which include mountains, deserts, lowlands, oceans, gulfs, bays, straits, rivers, lakes, islands, and other types of landforms. From there you add in layers of complexity, including the study of major cities, regions, languages, ethnicities, religions, and currencies. Next, become familiar with where natural resources and certain agricultural products are produced. Then add the historical highlights and political system of each country. Try to study at least a few hours a day to retain all the knowledge you have gained. Before you know it, you will start building a vast geographic encyclopedia inside your head!

Caitlin Snaring, 2006, 2007 State Bee Champion, Washington State (7th–8th Grade); 2007 National Champion (8th Grade)

••••••••••••••••••••••••••

Write everything down in notebooks then use them to quiz yourself a little bit each night. Make flashcards of countries and their capitals, territories and their capitals, countries and their currencies, and states and their nicknames. Fill out outline maps of the world, each continent, and each country. Read the newspaper everyday to brush up on your current events, and play geography trivia games on the Internet.

Make sure you make geography fun. But don't make the Bee about winning it all (even though it would be nice) or studying all the time. Get your friends involved in your studying. One of my best friends, who knows very little about geography, always quizzed me on whatever she could think of.

Olivia Colangelo, 2003 School Bee Champion (7th Grade); 2004 State Bee Champion, Pennsylvania (8th Grade)

● ●

My major tips for the Bee are to STAY CALM during the questions that you are asked, and close your eyes so that you can hear the questions better. Never panic. Just think calmly and coolly about each question. Even if you don't know the answer, most questions can be narrowed down to two choices. Then make an educated guess based on the clues in the question. Never cram the day before the Bee, and make sure to get a good night's sleep.

Krishnan Chandra, 2004–06 State Bee Champion, Massachusetts (6th–8th Grade)

● ●

Always make good use of your time, and study regularly. I studied three hours a day on weekdays and eight hours a day on weekends. Try not to just memorize but also to understand. If you can understand the world, this will help you to prepare not only for the Bee but also for a future career and for life.

Neeraj Sirdeshmukh, 2006 State Bee Champion, New Hampshire (8th Grade)

•••••••••••••••••••••••••••

I have always loved learning about people and places, so for me preparing for the Bee was a way to complement the knowledge I had already acquired. I enjoyed every minute I spent reading, poring over maps, memorizing facts, and playing geography-based computer games. My advice is simply to enjoy preparing while learning as much information as possible.

Tom Meyerson, 2003 and 2004 State Bee Champion, District of Columbia (7th and 8th Grades)

•••••••••••••••••••••••••••

I prepared for the Bee by having my family go through questions in the *National Geographic Bee Official Study Guide, Afghanistan to Zimbabwe,* and *The Geography Bee Complete Preparation Handbook,* looking at atlases, and watching TV programs, especially the History and Travel Channels. Before the competition, I contacted the previous state winner for New Jersey to see what tips he had.

Evan Meltzer, 2006 State Bee Champion, New Jersey (8th Grade)

CHAPTER **6**

Resources Genghis Khan Would Have Loved

Many centuries ago the great Mongol ruler, Genghis Khan, united his nomad tribes into a formidable army. His Golden Horde swept across the Central Asian steppe on horseback, terrorizing and plundering settlements from the Caspian Sea to the Pacific Ocean. They devastated cities, redirected rivers, and left deserts crowded with fleeing refugees. The Chinese built the Great Wall to keep the "barbarians" out, the Persians hid from them, and the Europeans fell like matchsticks. At the time of Genghis Khan's death in 1227, he controlled one of the greatest land empires the world has ever known.

Mr. Khan succeeded because, unlike the Europeans, his army did not wear heavy armor or burden itself with supply wagons that could break down. The Mongols traveled exceptionally light and fast. Their excellent use of geographic information made this possible. Mongol scouts went out months ahead of the main army, secretly gathering crucial information about terrain, vegetation, and settlements. This later assured the best routes, food for the men and ponies, and great hideaways. In a nutshell (or saddlebag), the Mongol scouts were simply the best.

Although great in the 13th century, Genghis's information was meager compared with what our current atlases, globes, and reference books can provide. Throw in television, the Internet, e-mail, and cell phones that allow instant information to flow around the globe, and you have an advantage that might have turned back even the Golden Horde.

The Mongols aside, just imagine how historic news headlines might have read if our current geographic information and communications technology had been available long ago. We might have seen: "GPS Navigation Guides Columbus to New World (film and details at 11:00)!" "Paul Revere E-Mails Alert from North Church!" "Custer's Lieutenant Faxes Map of Indian Camps." "Cell Phone Saves Captain Scott at South Pole."

The good news today is that for modest barter or a quick crusade to your local library, even ordinary peasants can obtain geographic learning materials the great Khan would have loved (and probably even killed for). An exhaustive list would make a book in itself, so this one simply highlights proven resources that will help you learn to think like a geographer.

ATLASES

Even if you're not scheming to plunder European villages, a good world atlas belongs in every ger, or yurt. This is the standard reference for Bee preparation and should include a full set of political, physical, and thematic maps (population, economic, climate, etc.). Also, look for country profiles, information about the oceans, plate tectonics, time zones, geographic comparisons, etc.

Our rapidly changing world alters the political landscape very quickly, so beware that if your atlas is more than five years old, some country names and boundaries may be outdated. The same is true for population figures and similar statistics. The rule of thumb is always to look for the most recent edition. Also, check to see if a less expensive paperback edition is available.

Large World Atlases

National Geographic Atlas of the World, 9th Edition.
National Geographic Society, Washington, DC, 2010.
A superb collection of political, physical, urban, regional, and ocean-floor maps; thematic maps covering topics such as climate patterns, plate tectonics, population, economic trends, and world cultures; country profiles; satellite imagery; temperature and rainfall; geographic comparisons; and a comprehensive index.

Midsize World Atlases

National Geographic Family Reference Atlas of the World, 3rd Edition. National Geographic Society, Washington, DC, 2009.
A comprehensive, family-friendly atlas with sections about the world, continents, oceans, and space. It includes an expansive thematic section with maps, graphs, charts, photographs, and an extensive list of geographic comparisons.

Rand McNally Goode's World Atlas, 22nd Edition.
Rand McNally & Co., Skokie, IL, 2009.
A comprehensive world atlas that includes a wide variety of thematic maps; world and regional maps; geographic comparison tables, and explanations of map scale, map projections, and Earth-Sun relationships.

National Geographic Collegiate Atlas of the World, 2nd Edition.
National Geographic Society, Washington, DC, 2011.
This detailed atlas features excellent world and regional maps. The many thematic maps (e.g., Health and Literacy, Defense and Conflict, Protected Lands) are a real strength.

Children's and Student World Atlases

National Geographic Student Atlas of the World, 3rd Edition.
National Geographic Society, Washington, DC, 2009. (Grades 6–10)
Packed with informative thematic maps that explore the world's physical and human systems, focusing on geology, climate, vegetation, population, economies, food, energy, and mineral resources. For each continent there are three sets of maps (physical and political, climate and precipitation, population and predominant economies) plus a photo essay. Web sites are included for finding additional information and updating statistics.

National Geographic Kids World Atlas, Paperback Edition (updated).
National Geographic Society, Washington, DC, 2010. (Grades 3–7)

Winner of the *Parents' Choice* Gold Award, this atlas contains world thematic maps, photo essays, satellite images, physical and political maps of each continent, country profiles, geographic comparisons, a glossary, and a comprehensive index. This latest edition has gone interactive, with its own Web site that provides links to a host of photos, videos, games, world music, animal sounds, maps, and more.

Specialty Atlases

National Geographic Atlas of the Middle East, 2nd Edition. National Geographic Society, Washington, DC, 2008.
Explores the complex history of the Middle East through maps devoted to topics that include the rise and falls of empires, civilizations, major conflicts, holy sites, and various other significant events that have shaped the region.

Ocean: An Illustrated Atlas. Sylvia A. Earle and Linda Glover. National Geographic Society, Washington, DC, 2008.
Features 300 detailed maps, photographs, and state-of-the-art satellite images. Includes details about climate, weather, currents, tides, and the ocean's living systems as well as essays by experts on topics from deep-sea drilling to predicting El Niño.

National Geographic United States Atlas for Young Explorers, 3rd Edition. National Geographic Society, Washington, DC, 2008.
Superb U.S., state, and regional maps explain the primary geographical relationships in the United States. Third edition features concise state profiles, photographic essays on each region and state, thematic

spreads on topics such as natural disasters, immigration, and climate change, and an interactive Web site that provides links to a host of National Geographic photos, videos, games, animal sounds, maps, and more.

National Geographic Atlas of China. National Geographic Society, Washington, DC, 2009.
Featuring more than 300 full-color maps and illustrations, this atlas provides provincial and city coverage, thematic maps on a wide range of topics, including trade, industry, military strength, tourism, religion, and languages, plus a historical time line and travel information.

Atlas of Global Development: A Visual Guide to the World's Greatest Challenges, 3rd Edition. World Bank Publications, Washington, DC, 2011.
Easy-to-read world maps, tables, and graphs highlight key social, economic, and environmental data for the world's economies. Topics include infant mortality, gross domestic product, femalelabor, drinking water, forest cover, and CO_2 emissions.

Student Atlas of World Politics, 9th Edition, McGraw/Dushkin, 2010.
Emphasizes current affairs that reflect recent developments in political geography and international relations. This collection of maps and data is particularly useful for exploring the relationships between geography and world politics.

GEOGRAPHIC REFERENCE BOOKS

Geography of Religion: Where God Lives, Where Pilgrims Walk. John Esposito, Susan Tyler Hitchcock, Desmond Tutu, and Mpho Tutu. National Geographic Society, Washington, DC, 2006.

This comprehensive reference traces each of the great religions of humankind from its ancient roots to its role in modern life.

National Geographic Almanac of Geography. National Geographic Society, Washington, DC, 2005.

A comprehensive, illustrated reference packed with easy-to-understand information about our physical world, human culture, and world economy. Hundreds of maps, charts, drawings, and photographs support the text.

Merriam-Webster's Geographical Dictionary, Revised 3rd Edition. Merriam-Webster, Inc., Springfield, MA, 2007.

Provides an alphabetical listing of more than 54,000 places and features, with concise information about each plus hundreds of maps and tables.

Geographica's World Reference. Laurel Glen Publishing, San Diego, CA, 2000.

Concise information divided into three comprehensive parts: Planet Earth, People and Society, and A–Z Country Listings. Many illustrations and an excellent gazetteer.

The National Geographic Bee Ultimate Fact Book: Countries A to Z. Andrew Wojtanik. National Geographic Society, Washington, DC, 2012.

This updated book is full of facts about 195 countries that the author compiled to help him study for and win the 2004 National Geographic Bee.

Our Fifty States. Mark H. Bockenhauer and Stephen F. Cunha. National Geographic Society, Washington, DC, 2004.

Organized by geographic regions, this book is packed with specially designed maps and concise essays that explore the history, climate, natural resources, and physical features of each region, state, the District of Columbia, and the territories.

ALMANACS

The World Almanac for Kids 2012. Sarah Janssen.
World Almanac Books, New York, NY, 2011.

Abundant information on essential topics, such as animals, computers, inventions, movies and television, religion, and sports. This fact book includes many photographs, illustrations, and maps, along with puzzles, brainteasers, and other activities.

The World Almanac and Book of Facts 2011. Sarah Janssen. World Almanac Books, New York, NY, 2010.

A classic annual with a price that drops during the year. Crammed with global facts from farm imports to volcanic activity and baseball batting averages.

National Geographic Almanac of World History, 2nd Edition. Patricia Daniels and Stephen G. Hyslop. National Geographic Society, Washington, DC, 2011.

Through essays, detailed maps, charts, and time lines, this book traces world history from the dawn of humanity to the 21st century.

National Geographic Kids Almanac 2012. National Geographic Society, Washington, DC, 2011.

This colorful page turner is packed with fun-to-browse features, useful reference material, homework help developed by educators, and quirky facts. Every chapter is updated annually with new content: animal photography; cool inventions; adventure; nature; maps of the continents; hundreds of facts and figures; and fascinating stories about incredible creatures, space, vacations, and more.

GEOGRAPHY TEXTBOOKS

Fourth- through eighth-grade social studies textbooks are a great source for learning about geography. As your skills improve, check out the textbooks for more advanced levels. Don't be afraid of college textbooks. Although they are more difficult to read, if you understand geography fundamentals, they offer a comprehensive and advanced tutorial on most topics. You can find these texts in bookstores, especially college and secondhand bookstores. Or surf the Internet for the best bargains (search under "used college textbooks"). College and university libraries shelve textbooks. Many state and community colleges will allow you to obtain a library card so you can borrow books. If a book was published in the last five years, check for a companion Web site with chapter summaries and a dizzying array of self-tests.

LITERATURE

Reading nonfiction books on just about any topic—exploration, sports, survival, wars, biography, even regional cookbooks!—can help expand your geographic knowledge. Even fiction has to have a setting, and most authors carefully research the background for their plots. This means that just about anything you read can add to your geographic knowledge.

CYBERSPACE RESOURCES

There are great stops on our rapidly emerging information superhighway. Beware that URL addresses change frequently. If you have trouble finding any, consult one of the popular Internet search engines, such as Google (www.google.com) or Lycos (www.lycos.com), and simply request the site name. In any search engine, entering key words such as geography games, geography facts, or geography maps, will produce an array of sites to explore and learn about our world.

Check out the main National Geographic Web site— www.nationalgeographic.com—or one of the following:

•www.nationalgeographic.com/wildworld: online atlas of world wildlife and ecosystems

•www.nationalgeographic.com/kids-world-atlas: the companion site to *National Geographic World Atlas for Young Explorers,* 3rd Edition

•www.nationalgeographic.com/geobee: a site that offers five new National Geographic Bee questions each day

UN Atlas of the Oceans: www.oceansatlas.org
An excellent source of readily accessible and up-to-the-minute information about oceans. Designed for government policy experts and students alike, this site provides information relevant to the sustainable development of the oceans, from basic explanations to intricate data sets.

Quintessential Instructional Archive: www.quia.com/dir/geo
Good flash card quiz site, with plenty of other interactive games. Click "Popular Categories" then navigate the pull-down menu to geography for dozens of worthy activities.

World Resources Institute: www.wri.org
Click on Climate & Energy, and People & Ecosystems.

About Geography: www.geography.about.com
This site offers free downloads and links to other geography sites, outline maps, and current events.

Population Reference Bureau: www.prb.org
The best source for world population, with interactive population pyramids, a quiz, recent news, country data, and links to other sites.

The CIA World Fact Book:

www.cia.gov/library/publications/the-world-factbook/index.html

Downloadable maps, current information, and background data on every country.

Science at NASA: www.earth.nasa.gov

Click "For Kids Only." This site explores air, water, land, and hazards at a level useful for Bee contestants.

United Nations: www.un.org

Full of country facts, statistics, current events, maps, and more.

Newspapers online: www.newspapers.com/index.htm
and library.uncg.edu/news

These two sites feature 7,000 links to all of the world's online newspapers and other sources of information. A great source for current events from a global perspective. Many are published in languages native to the region, but nearly every highly populated country and many regional papers offer an English edition.

Environment Canada: www.ec.gc.ca/sce-cew

Features useful material for Bee Kids. Click "Youth Zone" for links to educational resources and games. Presented in English and French!

GEOsources (the Canadian Geography Web site): www.ccge.org

Canada's top site to learn about its people and places. Offers quizzes.

National Atlas of Canada: www.atlas.gc.ca
Great technical information, maps, and educational materials.

California Geographical Survey World Atlas of Panoramic Images:
www.humboldt.edu/cga (click World Atlas)
Test your knowledge of mountains, rivers, peninsulas, and all the
rest—from space! Accurate and downloadable, this perspective is
very different from maps.

Google Earth: earth.google.com
Curious about what La Paz, the Nile River, or the Fedchenko Glacier
actually looks like from above? Google Earth takes you there. First,
download the free software, then use the images to build your mental
map of the world.

GREAT GEO GAMES
You'll find *GeoSpy, GeoBee Challenge* (also available as a board
game), and lots of other National Geographic geography games at:
kids.nationalgeographic.com/kids/games/geographygames

Carmen Sandiego. The Learning Company
This clever quiz game tests your geographic knowledge, from the
USA and beyond.

Brain Quest—Know the States Game. Educational Insights,
Rancho Dominguez, CA.
An entertaining board game that teaches locations, capital cities,
American culture, and scenic features for all 50 states.

Name That Country Game. Educational Insights,
Rancho Dominguez, CA.

A board game that uses names, salutations, or special features on postcards to help you identify countries and capitals. The game can be played at varying levels of difficulty and tests knowledge of rivers, major cities, languages, and currencies.

Go Travel: Africa, South America. Travel by Games, Clinton, IA.
These fun card games test your knowledge of history, geography, people, plants, animals, and problems on these continents.

GeoSafari Talking Globe. Educational Insights,
Rancho Dominguez, CA.

A talking geography quiz game and globe all in one. The 5,000-interactive-question database challenges players about their world knowledge. An advanced version offers 10,000 questions.

OTHER STUDY AIDS

Globes

Globes are available from a variety of manufacturers. Be sure to check the product date before ordering. Those produced by National Geographic can be found on the Society's Web site (www.nationalgeographic.com) or by calling 1-800-NGS-LINE.

Magazines

National Geographic magazine, *National Geographic Kids*, *National*

Geographic Explorer, Canadian Geographic, Time for Kids (TFK), and newsweeklies, such as *Time, Newsweek,* and *U.S. News & World Report,* include great articles, maps, graphs, and pictures.

Television
Programming on the National Geographic Channel, Public Television (*Nature, Bill Nye the Science Guy, Kratts' Creatures,* etc.), CNN, C-SPAN, the Discovery Channel, the History Channel, and nightly news broadcasts will greatly expand your world.

CD-ROMS
The National Geographic Society, Rand McNally, GeoSafari, Hammond, and George F. Cram offer many digital versions of their world atlases, picture libraries, and other specific topics (history, world regions, exploration, etc.). Be sure to check the operating system requirements before purchasing any software.

Blank Outline Maps
Free downloads are available online from the following:

National Geographic Xpeditions Atlas:
www.nationalgeographic.com/xpeditions/atlas

About Geography: geography.about.com/library/maps/blindex.htm

Arizona Geographic Alliance: alliance.la.asu.edu/azga

For a book of blank outline maps, contact the US Map and Book company (1-800-458-2306; www.usmapandbook.com).

*Our country's future
absolutely depends on
our ability to see
the connections
between ourselves and
our global neighbors.*
—GILBERT M. GROSVENOR
(2001), CHAIRMAN OF
THE BOARD, NATIONAL
GEOGRAPHIC SOCIETY

Note to Teachers

The National Geographic Society developed the National Geographic Bee in response to concern about the lack of geographic knowledge among young people in the United States. In a ten-country Gallup survey conducted for the Society in 1988 and 1989, Americans 18 to 24 (the youngest group surveyed) scored lower than their counterparts in the other countries. Shocked by such poor results, the National Geographic Society spearheaded a campaign to return geography to American classrooms. Since 1989, the Bee has been one of several projects designed to encourage the teaching and study of geography. With nearly five million fourth through eighth graders entering each year, the Bee is one of the nation's most popular academic contests.

Some parents and even a few teachers think the Bee might resemble an orderly Trivial Pursuit contest. Yet, in more than a decade of coordinating the California State Bee, I have not seen a single adult who arrives with that opinion leave with it intact. Indeed, kids who correctly answer questions on topics such as glacial erosion, Hinduism, location, and changing political blocks humble a new flock of adults every year. The annual assembly of teachers, parents, and media is impressed not just with what the contestants know right off the bat, but also with how they methodically answer questions that at first appear to stump them. This ability to think like a geographer—to integrate physical, cultural, and economic knowledge—shines through at every level of the Bee.

Teaching young people to think like geographers provides them with vital understanding of the connections that exist between ourselves, our global neighbors, and the physical environment that supports us all. The U.S. Congress has recognized this important role by designating geography as one of ten core academic subjects included in federal education acts that have been passed into law since 1994. Unfortunately, geography in the No Child Left Behind Act that was passed in 2001 lacks the designated funding mandates that accompany other core academic subjects. Ongoing efforts by the National Geographic Society and others seek to improve this situation so that teachers can receive the support they need to provide crucial geographic education.

The National Geographic Society also offers many forms of support to teachers who seek to enhance the geographic education they provide to students. The national K–12 geography standards, published as *Geography for Life: National Geography Standards*, are a comprehensive presentation of what students should know and be able to do as the result of their educational experiences. Accompanying these voluntary national standards is *Path Toward World Literacy: A Standards Based Guide to K–12 Geography*, which presents a scope and sequence for teaching geography along with explanations and activities that assist teachers, curriculum writers, parents, and the general public to effectively integrate the geography standards into the school curriculum. The National Geography Standards have been incorporated into the curriculum frameworks of almost all of the 50 U.S. states.

In addition to the national K–12 geography standards, the National Geographic Society has established a Geography Alliance Network—university partnerships with local K–12 schools—that has chapters in most U.S. states and provides training and support for educators. Whether teaching a stand-alone geography class or wishing to incorporate geography into other subjects such as history, science, or vocational education, teachers can tap into a wealth of resources through the Geographic Alliance Network. It offers opportunities for professional development training, ready-to-use lesson plans and other teaching resources, and interaction with a community of professionals at the local school, state, and university levels who provide the mentoring, contacts, assistance, and camaraderie that help to energize the daily task of teaching.

National Geographic also offers an education site and EdNet, an online community that provides education news, resources, discussion, and much more. Among the programs on EdNet, EarthCurrent News Digest contains links to bite-size news stories on classroom-perfect topics, such as archaeology and paleontology, exploration, peoples and cultures, plants and animals, science, and more. The education site provides links to maps, activities, and other programs for educators at National Geographic.

Contact information for schools to register for the Bee, obtain the geography standards, locate a state Alliance, or obtain online geography education information appears below. These are the perfect places to receive answers to your questions and to explore the world of possibilities in geography education.

Whether you are an experienced geo-educator or a newcomer, the Bee is a sure bet to stir student interest in the "Why of Where." Running the contest is simple. The Society provides registered schools with an instruction booklet, the questions and answers, certificates, and prizes. Think of the Bee as an open door to a world of fun and productive learning.

GEOGRAPHIC SUPPORT COORDINATES

To register for the National Geographic Bee

Principals of eligible U.S. schools can write to

National Geographic Bee
National Geographic Society
1145 17th Street N.W.
Washington, D.C. 20036-4688

*Principals in U.S. schools with students in grades four through eight must register their schools to participate in the Bee by a deadline, usually October 15. Principals may request registration by writing on school letterhead and enclosing a check, purchase order, or money order for $90 (U.S. funds; cost in 2012) made payable to the National Geographic Society. **The registration deadline is usually extended to December 15, but schools must pay a late fee if they miss the original deadline.** For the* *most current information, call 202-828-6659 or visit the Bee Web site, nationalgeographic.com/geobee.*

For information about the Canadian Geography Challenge go to

geochallenge.ca/geochallenge/register.asp

To find your state geographic alliance office and for other education resources, go to

nationalgeographic.com/education

To order Geography for Life: National Standards in Geography, contact

store.ncge.net/merchant2

To order Path Toward World Literacy, contact

The Grosvenor Center for Geographic Education
Southwest Texas State University
601 University Drive
San Marcos, TX 98666

www.geo.txstate.edu/grosvenor/publication.html

To order more copies of the fourth edition of *How to Ace the National Geographic Bee: Official Study Guide* or *The National Geographic Bee Ultimate Fact Book: Countries A to Z* (by 2004 Bee winner Andrew Wojtanik) go to www. ngchildrensbooks.com **or any place that books are sold.**

Answers

Round 1
1. Colorado
2. Virginia
3. Illinois
4. Alabama
5. Idaho
6. North Dakota
7. Maryland
8. Colorado
9. Arizona
10. Pennsylvania
11. Delaware
12. South Carolina

Round 2
1. Miami, Florida
2. Syracuse, New York
3. San Antonio, Texas
4. Spokane, Washington
5. Fresno, California
6. Asheville, North Carolina
7. San Juan, Puerto Rico
8. Las Vegas, Nevada
9. Green Bay, Wisconsin
10. Savannah, Georgia
11. Springfield, Missouri
12. Colorado Springs, Colorado

Round 3
1. Tanzania
2. Virginia
3. Ohio
4. Vermont
5. Kentucky
6. Idaho
7. Maine
8. South Carolina
9. Oklahoma
10. Oregon
11. Mississippi
12. North Dakota

Round 4
1. Africa
2. Asia
3. Australia

4.	Europe
5.	Antarctica
6.	South America
7.	Asia
8.	North America
9.	Africa
10.	South America
11.	Australia
12.	Europe

Round 5
1.	gulf
2.	elevation
3.	moraine
4.	tsunami
5.	mantle
6.	archipelago
7.	canopy
8.	trench
9.	iron
10.	mouth
11.	current
12.	butte

Round 6
1.	Romania
2.	Argentina
3.	Libya
4.	Philippines
5.	Dominican Republic
6.	Saudi Arabia
7.	Canada
8.	India
9.	Greece
10.	Mozambique

Round 7
1.	India
2.	Turkey
3.	Canada
4.	New Zealand
5.	India
6.	Mexico
7.	Kenya
8.	Iceland
9.	Madagascar
10.	Hungary

Tiebreaker Questions
1.	Madagascar
2.	Guam
3.	South Africa
4.	isthmus
5.	Black Sea
6.	Denmark
7.	Nicaragua
8.	Strait of Magellan

SCHOOL-LEVEL FINAL

Map Questions
1.	Wisconsin
2.	Tennessee
3.	Florida
4.	Nevada
5.	Colorado
6.	Pennsylvania
7.	North Carolina
8.	Iowa

QUALIFYING TEST

1. 2
2. 4
3. 2
4. 1
5. 4
6. 1
7. 2
8. 2
9. 1

Analogies
10. 3
11. 4
12. 4

Map Questions
13. 4
14. 1
15. 2
16. 1

STATE-LEVEL PRELIMINARY

Round 1
1. Florida
2. Nebraska
3. Kentucky
4. New Hampshire
5. California
6. Minnesota
7. South Dakota
8. Colorado
9. Arizona
10. Alaska
11. Maryland
12. North Carolina

Round 2
1. intermittent
2. seasonal
3. playa
4. lava dome
5. steppe
6. arête
7. geothermal
8. ladder
9. jet stream
10. kelp forest

Round 3
1. Ecuador
2. Volga River
3. Malaysia
4. Canterbury
5. Bermuda
6. Venice
7. Africa
8. Bangalore
9. Asia
10. Saudi Arabia
11. Andaman Sea
12. Cambodia

Round 4
1. Ontario
2. Guatemala
3. Vietnam
4. Kenya
5. Kazakhstan
6. Bulgaria
7. New Zealand
8. Democratic Republic of the Congo
9. Syria
10. Greece

Round 5
1. China
2. Australia
3. Spain
4. United Arab Emirates
5. Guinea
6. Singapore
7. Hungary
8. Israel
9. North Korea
10. United Kingdom

Round 6
1. California
2. Florida
3. Wisconsin
4. Hawaii
5. Vermont
6. Maryland
7. Alabama
8. Idaho
9. Nebraska
10. North Dakota

Round 7
1. Portugal
2. Algeria
3. Canada
4. Venezuela
5. Nigeria
6. Afghanistan
7. Slovenia
8. Argentina
9. Qatar
10. Nepal

Tiebreaker Questions
1. Turkey
2. Italy
3. Johannesburg
4. Hudson Bay
5. Bhutan
6. The Hague
7. Brazil
8. Uganda

STATE-LEVEL FINAL

Oral Analogies
1. Alaska
2. Sierra Nevada
3. Red River
4. Texas
5. Lake Huron
6. Florida
7. New York City
8. Tennessee
9. Wasatch Range
10. Rio Grande
11. Ohio River

Photo Questions
1. Vermont
2. Wyoming
3. Missouri
4. Oregon

Map Questions
1. Great Smoky Mountains National Park
2. Statue of Liberty National Monument

3.   Golden Gate National
              Recreation Area
4.   Mount Rushmore National
              Memorial

NATIONAL-LEVEL PRELIMINARY

Round 1
1.   Alexander Mackenzie
2.   Thor Heyerdahl

Round 2
1.   Kenya
2.   Indonesia

Round 3
1.   Pakistan
2.   Cuba

Round 4
1.   Spain
2.   The Bahamas

Round 5
1.   ice shelf
2.   basalt

Credits
p. 7, Brian Andreas's quote appears in *Geography*, by StoryPeople (www. storypeople.com); p. 11, Muhammad Ahmad Faris's quote appears in *The Home Planet,* conceived and edited by Kevin W. Kelly for the Association of Space Explorers, Addison-Wesley Publishing Company, New York, and Mir Publishers, Moscow; art p. 36, Shusei Nagaoka; p.92-93, photos courtesy of Google Earth; back cover: Rebecca Hale, National Geographic.

About the Author

Stephen F. Cunha is the chair and professor of geography at Humboldt State University in California. He is also the state coordinator for the National Geographic Bee and co-author of *Our Fifty States,* a children's reference book published by National Geographic. He and his family live near Redwood National Park.

Acknowledgments

Many talented people contributed to this book. Thanking Mary Hackett of the California Geographic Alliance for Russian around on our behalf requires a book in itself. I would have Ghana crazy without Mary Lee Elden, Megan Webster, Dan Malessa, Erin Dickinson, Geoffrey Hatchard, Tom Peyton, and Jo Erikson of the National Geographic Bee staff, who provided the questions. I would have Benin the dark about the Great Canadian Geography Challenge without Dale Gregory of Centennial School, British Columbia. Mary Cunha, geography lecturer at Humboldt State University, gave the entire manuscript a good Czech. The Bee kids who are the Seoul of Chapter 5 were totally cool. I also thank many young readers for sending me great suggestions—Ural great! Most important, I Congo on and on about Suzanne Patrick Fonda, Rebecca Baines, and Priyanka Lamichhane of National Geographic Children's Books. Now that we are Finnish, I hope it makes you Hungary to learn Samoa geography!

The National Geographic Society is one of the world's largest nonprofit scientific and educational organizations. Founded in 1888 to increase and diffuse geographic knowledge, the Society works to inspire people to care about the planet. National Geographic reflects the world through its magazines, television programs, films, music and radio, books, DVDs, maps, exhibitions, live events, school publishing programs, interactive media and merchandise. *National Geographic* magazine, the Society's official journal, published in English and 33 local-language editions, is read by more than 38 million people each month. The National Geographic Channel reaches 320 million households in 34 languages in 166 countries. National Geographic Digital Media receives more than 15 million visitors a month. National Geographic has funded more than 9,400 scientific research, conservation and exploration projects and supports an education program promoting geography literacy. For more information, visit nationalgeographic.com.

For more information, please call 1-800-NGS LINE (647-5463) or write to the following address:
National Geographic Society
1145 17th Street N.W.
Washington, D.C. 20036-4688 U.S.A.